RESTORATION OF MEN:
God's Rescue of Women and Children

- **Prophetic Restoration of Manhood**

- **Accountability**

Karl M. Duff

Destiny Image Publishers
P.O. Box 351
Shippensburg, PA 17257

"Speaking to the Purposes of God for this Generation"

ISBN 1-56043-022-2

For Worldwide Distribution
Printed in the U.S.A.

First Printing: 1990
Second Printing: 1994

Destiny Image books are available through these fine distributors outside the United States:

Christian Growth, Inc.
Jalan Kilang-Timor, Singapore 0315

Lifestream
Nottingham, England

Rhema Ministries Trading
Randburg, South Africa

Salvation Book Centre
Petaling, Jaya, Malaysia

Successful Christian Living
Capetown, Rep. of South Africa

Vision Resources
Ponsonby, Auckland, New Zealand

WA Buchanan Company
Geebung, Queensland, Australia

Word Alive
Niverville, Manitoba, Canada

Inside the U.S., call toll free to order:
1-800-722-6774

CONTENTS

To Gretchen,
my nourisher and healer,
the portrait of a godly woman;
and to all those who have passed through fire
for the sake of the bride of Jesus Christ.

PREFACE

In a society fast disintegrating, it is easy to find a host of culprits. Drugs, sexual promiscuity, television, unfaithfulness and a permissive society only begin to hint at the variety of causes and symptoms to which we may attribute the lawlessness and destruction now rapidly taking place. This increased enemy activity is a sign of the end times and marks the approach of the return of the Lord Jesus Christ. Should we yearn for our more rapid destruction that He might return the sooner? Can anything be done in the time remaining? What are the demands upon us? What will be the precepts of the millennium? What must be laid in place for those "not uninformed," who are to "be ready" for the return of Christ?

Do we not know that the responsibility for the preparation of the bride is the bride's and not the bridegroom's (Col. 1:24, Rev. 19:7-8)?

Many are the women who sense that under all the foolishness of their husbands is a true man. Blessed are the few who know that, without their manipulation and devices, God has a plan and precepts for the stripping off of the foolish boy and the revealing of the true man. Many are the daughters who dream of romance, sexual and family fulfillment with their knight in shining armor — a man who will be true for the rest of their lives. Blessed are the few who know that God gives them these visions and that He has a plan to deliver and prepare such a man through the prescriptions of their earthly fathers. How blind these women are to their own foolishness and to their godly role in contributing to their husbands' manhood!

Manhood is fast disappearing. The root cause of the destruction of women, families and children, the destruction of our nation, is the failure of men. They do not understand or seem to have the capacity to live for the purposes and functions for which God designed them. Women contribute to the problem; but it is consequential to the failure of their own fathers and husbands. Women can never be successful and fulfilled in the things for which God created them until men are successful in their role. But they play a vital part if they understand and apply God's Word to their own lives in harmony with God's precepts in the lives of their fathers, husbands and sons.

How can we deliver our sons and daughters to fulfillment in their lives? What are God's purposes in the design of a man? What are they in the design of a woman? How do men and women relate to reflect the image, character, personality and glory of God? How do they relate to illustrate the gospel to our children?

God's Word has answers! We were designed and created by a divine Creator for happiness and fulfillment. When we understand how we were designed, we can work in harmony with God's plan for our fulfillment. Within each man is the desire to be successful and to be a true man of God. As we are armed with God's Word, prayer and commitment, God has provided for our success and fulfillment, doing the things for which He designed us, living in victory and protection even while the world around us may be falling apart. Let us learn and apply His precepts and be found faithful when He returns.

Where sin increases, grace abounds all the more (Rom. 5:20).

PART I: HEALING

RESTORATION
TO THE RAVAGED

He sent His word and healed them.

Psalm 107:20

Therefore you will joyously draw water from the springs of salvation.

Isaiah 12:3

The Creation of Man and Woman

Then God said, "Let Us make man in Our image,
according to Our likeness..."

Genesis 1:26

Nearly everyone is familiar with the biblical story of creation, but we frequently gloss over a paradox that exists right at the outset. After creating the universe, the earth and all that dwells therein, God created Adam and established his authority over everything on the earth. God viewed all that He had created at the end of the sixth day and declared it to be "very good" (Gen. 1:31).

Placed in the Garden of Eden to cultivate and keep it, Adam named all the living creatures and was in perfect harmony with God. Yet it was not long before God said, "It is not good for the man to be alone; I will make him a helper suitable for him" (Gen. 2:18).

Wait a minute!

Didn't God declare everything He made to be "good"? Doesn't this mean perfect? Isn't it true that God had created man in His own image? That means he had the likeness of God, right? Since this takes place before the fall of man, that must mean Adam was without defect. Why does God then judge that it is not good for Adam to be alone?

This is the paradox.

How does one reconcile God's Word that He had created man in His own image and declared him to be "very good" with His ensuing statement that "It is not good for man to be alone"?

The answer lies in God's view of perfection.

The Hebrew word for "alone" in Genesis 2:18 is *bad.* It means "separated" or "solitary." God's statement reveals that He does not regard a solitary individual, regardless of his other attributes, as perfect, because he is solitary. God has a higher order of perfection that is expressed in His idea of composite unity, which in Hebrew is *echad. Echad* is a word for "one" which has been made from the verb *achad*, which means "to unify" or "to collect." Hence, *echad* is a word which means a composite whole made up of parts. It is actually a plural word. It is the same word that is used to describe a marriage (Gen 2:24), a group of people or a tribe (Gen 34:16) or a cluster of grapes (Num. 13:23).

Echad is the word that is used in Deuteronomy 6:4, where Moses says, "Hear, O Israel! The LORD is our God, the LORD is *one!*" The Godhead is comprised of the Father, the Son and the Holy Spirit. Each is identical in attributes (nature, character, power, etc.) but each does not have the same function.

It is this difference in functions that is the critical point here. God desired to raise Adam to a form similar to that of the Godhead, in which his functions would be divided, but his essence and perfection would remain unchanged, the idea being that he would enjoy a higher level of fulfillment and completeness by being in unity not only with God, but also with another human being with whom he lived intimately and in harmony "as one."

So God took His perfect creation of Adam and completed him. He raised him to a higher level of perfection by dividing him and creating a composite body and the relationship between man and woman. In so doing, God left the individual Adam no longer the same as he had been. Eve was removed and was also made different than Adam. Though equal in soul and spirit and equal before God, they were not identical with one another. They were separated to perform different functions.

We have analogies to help us to see this truth. Air in our lungs is different than air in a tire; the air is the same, but the functions of the air are different. The functions are determined by the vessels in which the air is placed.

Man and woman were created as dissimilar vessels for different, complimentary functions.

The Separation of Man and Woman

And God created man in His own image, in the image
of God He created him; male and female He created them.
Genesis 1:27

That the male and female functions were both in Adam upon creation is evident in the above verse. There was already a plurality in one flesh. In God's decision to separate the two, He moved to establish the same form of relationship between male and female as that which existed between man and God; one which was to be voluntary and not coerced, based upon love and not physical constraints. The question now arises, "What was the division of functions of male and female which God separated into man and woman?"

God describes in spectacular manner His own chief functional characteristics. These are the functions to which He gives preeminence in His teaching and in His relationships with man. Ahead of what has been reported to be over a hundred names by which God describes Himself throughout the Bible, there are two functional names which are given preeminence.

The first place in the Bible at which God describes Himself as having any functional form or characteristic is in His relationship with Abram when He appeared to Abram and said in a vision, "Do not fear, Abram, I am a shield to you. Your reward shall be very great" (Gen. 15:1).

This event took place some time after Abram had been obedient to God to leave his homeland and go to Canaan, and immediately after he took a risky action to honor God as the sole Source of his wealth. He refused to take any of the spoil of the kings of Shinar, whom he had just defeated. In so doing, he scorned the king of Sodom and his power to either protect Abram or to turn against him for publicly rebuking his offer of the spoils of the victory. God confirmed Himself with Abram by telling him that He Himself was Abram's shield and that Abram's reward would be very great.

God does not choose words frivolously. When He said, "I am a shield to you," God was not trying to approximate an idea. True, He was clearly stating that He was Abram's Protector. But He was not merely affirming this. There are many words which God could have chosen instead to imply protection, such as "roof," "wall," "clothing," "fortress," "arm," etc.(most of which are used elsewhere in Scripture to describe God). However, the word "shield" has particular additional connotations which we must understand.

A shield is an article of war used to receive mortal blows.

A shield is placed between the intended victim and the mortal enemy to take onto itself the blow that is intended for the destruction of the life of the victim.

A shield does not merely ward off the blow; it *receives* the blow *instead* of the victim.

A shield is damaged as a result of receiving the blow and must be repaired if it is to remain useful.

It is also noteworthy that God's serving the function of our shield is also given preeminence in the Book of Psalms as the first description of God given by the Psalmist. In Psalm three David prayed to God, saying, "But Thou, O Lord, art a shield about me..."

In Psalm two, in a Messianic prophecy, the Lord also reveals that there is One, "a Son," to whom all the nations must render homage, and that "blessed are all" who take refuge in Him. This is also significant both to the beginning of Psalms and to implying God's description of Himself as a shield.

Following Genesis 15:1, the second place in Scripture in which God gives Himself a specific title is in Genesis chapter seventeen, where He describes Himself as *El Shadday (shad-dah'ee),* translated into English as "God Almighty." Here God says, "I am God Almighty; walk before Me, and be blameless. And I will establish My covenant between Me and you, and I will multiply you exceedingly" (Gen. 17:1-2). At this point God also changes Abram's name to Abraham (father of a multitude), "For I will make you the father of a multitude of nations" (Gen. 17:5).

The context for this promise is the fruitful multiplication of Abraham's seed. God gives Abraham the covenant of circumcision and promises that Sarah will bear a son "at this season next year." Reproduction is the center of the subject.

The word *Shadday* is composed of two parts: *shad,* meaning "breast" as in the breast of a woman, and *day (da'hee),* meaning "able; ability, (more than) enough, sufficient, too much, very." By adding this suffix to the word "breast," God is saying that He is the all-sufficient, superlative and capable Supplier of life and everything that is represented by the woman's breast. This title is given at precisely the time God is about to fulfill His promise to Abraham and clarifies that the promised son is to be borne forth from Abraham's wife, as opposed to his maid Hagar, through whom he bore Ishmael (Gen. 17:15-19). At this time also, God changes Sarai's name to "Sarah," meaning "Princess."

We see, therefore, that in chapter seventeen of Genesis, God is highlighting the fulfillment of the promise through the wife (which Hebrew word is also related to the same roots as *Shadday*) and is identifying Himself with her as well as demonstrating His sufficiency to accomplish anything associated with reproducing, nourishing and sustaining the life He has promised.

Hence, we see that in His walk with Abraham, God determined that the most relevent functional descriptions related to Himself and the promises He had given him were those of a Shield and a Breast.

It is these two functions which were drawn apart when God resolved to give Adam a helpmate and to perfect Him in the likeness of God. In removing the rib from Adam, He withdrew the functions of the breast and placed them in Eve. He left the functions of the shield in Adam.

3

The Shield and The Breast

This is now bone of my bones, and flesh of my flesh; She shall be called Woman, because she was taken out of Man.

Genesis 2:23

Men and women were designed for mutually supporting and interdependent functions. Without a spouse, each is inherently incomplete, missing something essential for life which God intended to be provided through the other.

God has designed the woman to serve as a breast, the man as a breastplate.

Men need a source of nourishment and healing, inherently missing from their own bodies, natures and temperament. Restoration is essential for a damaged shield. Woman have the capacity to provide this, but themselves need a source of protection and covering, which is inherently missing from the breast. Protection of the breast is essential if it is to be successful in its life function. How strongly these two functions work to provide mutual benefit!

We see the outline of the functions of the woman in the work of her body and breast milk in supporting life. From the moment of conception, she begins to pour out her body on behalf of the baby, providing it with all its life resources from her own blood. At birth, her body switches immediately to the production of breast milk containing not only the nourishment for the continued growth of the baby, but also the antibodies for the protection of its health. Less evident perhaps, but of even greater overall importance is her nourishing and healing of the man who gives her the security in which she can safely raise their child.

In the design of the man God has provided all the inherent capabilities to serve as the woman's shield. We see this in his physiology and temperament. From his earliest age of interaction with contemporaries, a boy's natural temperament is given to confrontation and contesting. His body is designed for receiving blows and responding to attack. Relative to the woman, he is more emotionally and physically suited for conflict and less susceptible to the damage resulting.

As a shield, God intends the man to be the source of physical security, economic security and emotional security, subjects which will be further reviewed in light of Scripture.

Contrasting to the manner in which the woman's blood is poured out for nourishment and healing, his is to be poured out in defending, providing and protecting. He may be required at any time to yield his body or life to protect his family physically.

In addition and related to this, the man has been designed to be the economic provider, to build or provide shelter, to procure food and obtain all the other raw materials needed for a successful home. Over the span of his life, this is the manner in which most of his resources will be consumed.

Finally, the man is responsible for the emotional security of the woman. He is responsible to take onto himself all those things which can destroy her peace of mind, her perceptions of security in him, her reputation in the community and position in the home. He is to be an emotional shield, taking onto himself the things which would threaten her.

In the design of the woman, God has provided for every type of restoration and well-being of the man and their offspring. She is essentially non-confrontational. She prepares the food he has procured, she feeds his eyes, senses and body with things that delight his soul. She arranges the home decor, determines diet, clothing, hygiene, family festivities and administers the family "hearth," the very wellspring of the family's life. Relative to her husband, she does not get ill easily and has a capacity to minister health to her family despite her own condition. She delights in doing these things in the cradle of her husband's security.

She is also the chief life-giver in sexual fulfillment, the well from which her husband drinks and receives nourishment (Prov. 5:15), of which we will speak more later.

Since this is God's design, we may be confident that God has provided for fulfillment and blessing for those who apply their lives in harmony with their design and life purpose, the man in pouring out his life to protect the family from the forces which would destroy them from without, the woman in pouring out her life to nourish and heal her husband and children from within.

One of the main reasons we see so much catastrophe around us is that there are many men failing in the things for which they were designed and many women who are also failing because they are attempting to do things in their husbands' and fathers' place — things for which they were not designed.

It is clear that things have gone wrong with God's original creation, cataclysms from which we now struggle to recover. This catastrophe occurred with the fall of man. Many of the above-outlined functions of the shield and the breast commenced or became more complex consequent to the fall. But apparently the enemy was there all along and God's design was made to deal with him.

It is instructive to see the harmony of God's design even in the events that brought about the fall and brought the world to its present condition, and to appreciate the congenital defects which now mar our design as a result.

The Failure of the Shield and the Breast

Now the serpent was more crafty than any beast of the field which the LORD God had made.

Genesis 3:1

In the third chapter of Genesis, God describes the events which resulted in the death of man and the usurpation of God's creation. The one who is described as "more crafty than any beast of the field which the LORD God had made" planned to accomplish his purpose by first approaching Eve. She was found without a shield.

We are often left to wonder about such things as Eve's separation from Adam at the time of satan's approach. Were they under instruction to stay together? Was it only a separation of spirit? Was this a normal situation bound to arise eventually, given the freedom of Adam and Eve to do anything without sin except eat of the tree of the knowledge of good and evil? Or had the stage been set in some manner to open them up to the evil one?

What we can see is that Eve was indeed susceptible to deception for having been exposed from her covering. We might also perceive, based upon the experiences of sin in our own lives as well as that of Eve, that, once we have succumbed to sin, the weakness in our nature that entertained that sin becomes further weakened. We become more susceptible to repeat the sin than before. Acid corrodes. Limestone erodes before water to form caves. In the same way, creatures of darkness work to enlarge their habitat within our fallen natures.

Eve entertained satan's temptation and became permanently perverted in her tendencies to expose herself from under protective covering, her susceptibility to deception and the ease in which she can pass it on to her husband. The woman has become easy prey for those who would sweet talk her, pretending that they are acting for her best interests while lying in order to gain their own selfish and perverted goals (2 Tim. 3:6). She is not designed to resist, but to nourish. She has need of a shield from birth to death, first her father and then her husband, to protect her and her vital interests from destruction.

Where was Adam? Was he off doing his own thing? Did he unwittingly fail by leaving her exposed? What motivated him to repeat Eve's offense, even though according to Scripture "...it was not Adam who was deceived, but the woman..." (1 Tim. 2:14)? Was it possibly out of a sense of love for her (or a desire to exhibit love for her) that had transcended his love for God? Possibly it was his dependence upon whatever she gave him for nourishment. For when Eve saw "that the tree was good for food, and that it was a delight to the eyes, and that the tree was desirable to make one wise, she took from its fruit and ate; and she gave also to her husband with her, and he ate" (Gen. 3:6).

Now Adam's weakness, too, became permanently perverted. The man is now congenitally defective in his weakness and susceptibility to improper nourishment. He is a helpless babe, dependent upon his mother for food and healing until this responsibility is taken over by his wife. He is a sucker for lies regarding his true needs for nourishment and will frequently "take the bait" for things offered which work instead to his destruction.

Having been created with mutual dependencies, the fall of Adam and Eve has led them to an even greater degree of dependency, with all the defects of nature and lies of the enemy now working against us. However, the fall accomplished some good things. Through it, God has exposed the enemy, his nature and devices. Our mutual dependence as men and woman is crystal clear. And from God's promise to send "the seed of woman" to bruise (crush, strike) the serpent's head, we know we have God working on our behalf to restore us. He is arming us for victory with the truth. In the deepest part of our spirits, He helps us to recognize the truth.

Consider the popular modern parable of the beautiful girl who is accosted by the crude bully (perhaps a football player who has taken a crush on one of the cheerleaders). What is the scenario? It commences when he embarrasses her publicly by attempting to press his affections upon her, or perhaps he attempts to force her to give in to his advances. How does it proceed?

This is about the point where the "A" student from math class comes upon the scene, right? He weighs about 120 lbs. and wears Coke bottles for glasses. What does he do? Don't we all recognize the story? In the midst of many others who could have come to her aid, it is this man who steps in to defend her. "Leave her alone," he says, or words to that effect. What does he get for his trouble? We all know. Even our children know.

He gets broken. He winds up on the floor bloodied, with his glasses in pieces and perhaps his teeth and face, too. But this is only part of the story. There is more. There is the cheerleader's reaction.

How does the girl respond to this intercession on her behalf and its result? What does she do and why? She responds with an unrestrained outpouring of nourishment and healing for the broken warrior. She does this because in her heart of hearts, as with all women, she is looking for a man who is willing to be broken on her behalf. When she finds a man who gives her such a position of priority in his life, at this price, her heart is unlocked. She responds with her love.

This story's humor has been exploited any number of times in books and movies. One of the underlying reasons for its effectiveness and humor is because it accurately reflects the truth. This story is essentially indistinguishable in its key features from the story of the intercession of the Lord Jesus Christ for His bride. Everyone for whom He has interceded and whom He has called sees, understands and responds to His love expressed in His purchase price (John 3:16). He has purchased us with His broken body and His blood. What we would have never responded to in only empty words becomes reality through the redemptive power of His blood shed on our behalf.

There is a perverted version of this story also. The James Bond worshipers would have us believe that the hero immediately fornicates with the woman he has saved. No regard is given to his being in a covenant relationship with her. There is power to this perversion because it too contains elements of truth regarding the bonding which results from the man's efforts and the woman's response. However, this story is mixed with lies which would actually destroy the relationship. Satan uses incorrectly the sexual aspect of the relationship to pervert the truth and destroy the things which God intends for our blessing.

Things like "blood" and "death" on our behalf, and the picture of Christ giving Himself up for His Church (Eph. 5:25-29), draw us closer to the picture God has for us in understanding the nature of the places He has designed for men and women in marriage.

A Man's Man: A Study of Boaz and Ruth

Then the women said to Naomi, "Blessed is the LORD who has not left you without a redeemer today, and may his name become famous in Israel."

Ruth 4:14

Boaz' name has indeed become famous. He is in the family geneology of Jesus Christ. And, far more than any other man whose story is recorded in the Bible, he illustrates in his life the functions of the kinsman-redeemer and the characteristics of a godly man walking in right relationship with a woman. He is a scriptural "bank account" from which we may draw many riches to furnish ourselves. He reflects the splendor of manhood.

God is a Pattern-maker. In Boaz we have, not only the pattern pointing to Christ in the redemption of His Church, but the pattern showing us how we should walk as men on earth in our relationship with women.

In the Book of Leviticus, God set forth the law regarding redemption of either property or relatives fallen into the bondage of indebtedness. If it is property, "...his nearest kinsman is to come and buy back what his relative has sold" (Lev. 25:25). If it is a person who has sold himself as a slave, "One of his brothers may redeem him, or his uncle, or his uncle's son, may redeem him, or one of his blood relatives from his family may redeem him..." (Lev. 25:48-49) In addition, God provided for the redemption of a family name, in event of a husband's death, by requiring the husband's brother to do the duty of a brother-in-law with the deceased man's wife by taking her as his own wife and raising up the first son in his dead brother's name (Deut. 25:5-10). It is these principles which we see Boaz carrying out in the Book of Ruth. He ultimately married her after carrying out the functions of a kinsman-redeemer.

But first consider Ruth. Ruth was a foreigner who had married one of the sons of Elimelech and Naomi, Jews who during hard times had left Judea to live in Moab. Eventually, Elimelech and both his sons died while still living in Moab, leaving Naomi, Ruth and the other daughter-in-law, Orpah, as widows. After some discussion, Orpah decided to stay in her homeland with her relatives. But Ruth declared, "Do not urge me to leave you or turn back from following you; for where you go, I will go, and where you lodge, I will lodge. Your people shall be my people, and your God, my God. Where you die, I will die, and there I will be buried. Thus may the LORD do to me, and worse, if anything but death parts you and me" (Ruth 1:16-17).

There is a mystery here. Regardless of the lessons taught in the Book of Ruth regarding the power of a godly man to bring a woman into fulfillment in her life as a wife and mother, there is the pervading essence of another message also; it is hard to grasp or define, but tangibly present. It is the power of a godly woman to draw out the best in a man.

If there is anything evident about Ruth, it is that the reputation of her goodness and faithfulness had preceded her before she ever met Boaz. Women, never underestimate the power of your purity, goodness and faithfulness. It is one of the most powerful forces on earth!

When Naomi and Ruth returned to Bethlehem, they were destitute. It was the beginning of the barley harvest and Ruth, under Naomi's covering guidance and permission, went out into the fields to glean. The Scriptures give marvelous insight into the characters of both Ruth and Boaz.

It so happened that Ruth began to work in the field of Boaz, a relative of Elimelech, and that early on Boaz himself also happened to show up. He immediately inquired as to who she was and was informed that she was "the young Moabite woman who returned with Naomi from the land of Moab" (Ruth 2:6).

After it had been explained to Boaz that she had asked permission to glean, Boaz took two significant steps. He told his servants "not to touch" her. Then he told her not to go and glean in any other fields, but to "stay here with my maids" (Ruth 2:8). *He thus took concrete steps to provide for her physical protection.*

That Boaz also feared God and viewed providential encounters in terms of God's economy is also evident in his reply to Ruth regarding why he should show her such favor. He explained it in terms of her faithfulness to Naomi and her favor with God. He said, "May the LORD reward your work, and your wages be full from the LORD, the God of Israel, under whose wings you have come to seek refuge" (2:12).

Following the mealtime, when she rose to glean, Boaz commanded his servants, saying, "Let her glean even among the sheaves, and do not insult her. And also you shall purposely pull out for her some grain from the bundles and leave it that she may glean, and do not rebuke her" (2:15-16). She went home with an ephah of barley (about a half bushel)! In providing for Ruth far more grain than she needed, *we thus see Boaz also took concrete steps to provide for her economic security.*

We might pause here to note that Ruth was not without attraction to the younger men in the fields, to the extent that she did not report accurately to her mother-in-law Boaz' instructions to her. As she reported it to Naomi, she said that Boaz had advised her to stay close to his young men or servants. However, Naomi picked up on this right away and reworded the correct guidance to Ruth: "It is good, my daughter, that you go out with his maids, lest others fall upon you in another field." After this, Ruth got it right and followed this guidance (2:21-23).

By the end of the barley harvest, Naomi had come to some conclusions and, perhaps with some discernment regarding Boaz' character and godliness, put Ruth up to one of the riskiest ventures we can imagine. She told Ruth to bathe, dress up in her prettiest clothes, put on her best perfume and go down to the men's workplace, the threshing floor, in the middle of the night after the men had finished eating and drinking, and sleep at Boaz' feet (3:1-4)!

This amounts to one of us advising our daughter to dress provocatively and go with no protection in the middle of the night to a workplace where all the men have gone to sleep off their evening festivities down at the local tavern! A risky proposition, indeed!

It is hard to say just how discerning Naomi was. Since the fall, women have been marked with the tendency to "urge on, compel and manipulate" men, especially their husbands (Gen. 3:16). Was Naomi discerning enough to think she could safely advise Ruth of this undertaking, or did she anticipate that she could entrap Boaz and that his conscience would cause him to marry Ruth? How many women have followed this line of thought regarding marriage? In any event, it turned out well. Ruth carried out the instructions of her mother-in-law and found out that Boaz was not an average man.

In the middle of the night, he woke up and found this beautiful creature sleeping at his feet. He asked who she was and she immediately propositioned him in terms that could not be misunderstood. "I am Ruth your maid. So spread your covering over your maid, for you are a close relative [i.e., kinsman-redeemer]" (3:9).

Boaz was swept off his feet, although perhaps not in the fashion that Ruth expected. Boaz was more than flattered. He was uplifted and enhanced as a man to discover that this woman whom he had been protecting and providing for would consider him above many younger and more attractive men. And he still had his mind locked upon the LORD, whom he mentions in his first response, "May you be blessed of the LORD, my daughter. You have shown your last kindness to better than the first by not going after young men, whether poor or rich" (3:10).

How many men are there who at a moment like that could further act for the protection of a girl in whom they had invested considerable time and money to safeguard? How many are even aware of the devastating destruction that the response of a natural man would cause — or the eternal loss of priceless things for the sake of gratifying immediate desires? God is showing us that such virtue is possible. Boaz goes on to say further, " And now, my daughter, do not fear. I will do for you whatever you ask, for all my people in the city know that you are a woman of excellence" (3:11). He then commits to becoming her kinsman-redeemer, if another closer relative does not want to do so (thereby showing that he had already been thinking about it and had probably fallen in love with Ruth). With that commitment to walking the godly road of redemption, he risked not only losing the long-term promise *but also* the short-term gratification of Ruth's love. It was all or nothing.

In taking this position, Boaz was walking in God's redemptive principles for restoring the name, position and property of all who have fallen into bondage. In particular, he was carrying out the principles which his ancient relative, Judah, had refused to entrust to God in the case of his youngest son and Tamar, the widow of his eldest son, seven generations earlier. Judah had got it wrong, leading to incest and illegitimate children. Boaz got it right, thereby opening the door to promises that may have been deferred seven generations earlier through Judah's disobedience. Praise God for men like Boaz!

Then, as if it could not yet be evident that Boaz was paying a tremendous price himself on Ruth's behalf, he issued this order, "Let it not be known that a woman came to the threshing floor" (3:14). He thereby completed his actions to protect her reputation *and provide for her emotional security.*

With this, Boaz had carried out specific actions in all three primary areas alloted to men in their functions as shields over the women they would marry, both before and after they come into the marriage covenant. He still had risks to run, but in God's economy, Boaz had already secured the prize. He had gone through fire and water. He had become bonded to Ruth in his soul. How could God deny him?

We know little of Boaz' self-assurance or lack of it when he approached the elders at the gates of the city to inquire of the closest relative as to whether he would redeem the piece of land that went with Naomi and Ruth. There is drama every step of the way. At first the man says, "Yes!" But when he discovers he must also marry Ruth he makes a decision as short-sighted as Judah's many years earlier. He decides it would jeopardize his own inheritance if he were to raise a son in someone else's name. In front of all the elders of the city, he says, "No!" Boaz then declares the agreement in front of the witnesses and finishes, "...Moreover, I have acquired Ruth the Moabitess, the widow of Mahlon, to be my wife in order to raise up the name of the deceased on his inheritance, so that the name of the deceased may not be cut off from his brothers or from the court of his birthplace; you are witnesses today" (4:1-10) .

The effective man Boaz has now brought his bride Ruth into the place of her blessing. In the sanctity of the marriage covenant she receives the seed of her bridegroom. She becomes bonded to him in the giving of her life to him, responding to the life he has already given for her. She gives birth to new life, a son called Obed. The women rejoice in the things that women rejoice over, the lives of their husbands and children. They say to Naomi, "Blessed is the LORD who has not left you without a redeemer today, and may his name become famous in Israel. May he also be to you a restorer of life and a sustainer of your old age; for your daughter-in-law, who loves you and is better to you than seven sons, has given birth to him" (4:14-15) .

The Book of Ruth ends on a rather strange note. It cites ten generations, commencing with Perez and ending with David. Why would the Word of God record this particular short stretch of genealogy? Why in this particular place? Can you discern its significance?

We will take up this question in a later chapter.

6

Problems in the Ministry of the Shield

*Consider what I say, for the Lord will give you
understanding in everything.*
Second Timothy 2:7

All of us men have "multapul defecs"! We all fall short of the glory of God (Rom. 3:23). This is especially true, too, in our effectiveness as shields. Many of the areas in which we fall short are easily evident to others around us, but not to ourselves. Many faults are common to all.

One of the important things we should recognize (but normally do not) is that our wives were not designed for confrontation, especially with men. They were designed for ministering mercy and nourishment. Hence, we are asking for trouble, and usually get it, when we as husbands ask our wives to undertake something which is likely to involve confrontation with other men.

A good example is a husband who asks his wife to take the car in to the garage to have some work done on it. Unless the work to be done is well defined and previously approved by the husband, he is setting a course for certain difficulty, likely to compound his original error. His original error is in sending his wife to get the job done in the first place.

A car that goes in for a tune-up will likely come home with a new carburator. One bald tire could get you four new ones complete with new valve stems! A weak battery or voltage regulator problem may lead quickly to a car that has had its generator, starter motor and a few other things replaced, to which the husband would not have agreed. It is not abnormal at all for a $50 piece of work to result in a $250 bill that has already been paid when the husband comes home from work! He feels he's been cheated and takes his anger out on his wife. Recognize the problem? There are countless couples who identify with it.

The roots of the problem are these:

1) It is the husband's design and responsibility to be the family's agent in dealing in these types of matters, not the wife's. Dealing with men in a man's world (especially in which the wife is not expert) is likely to produce confrontational issues in which she will lose, because she naturally avoids them.

2) The husband is the shield for the family's economic security. When the family is defrauded the husband will discern and react more strongly than the wife.

3) The husband will react with much more anger when the underlying cause of the family's being defrauded is his fault, because he sent his wife to do his job. Hence, he is the cause of the loss. His spirit convicts him of his failure. But since he usually cannot see his personal responsibility, he blames his wife and takes his anger out on her.

This is an example of a "double or triple whammy." The husband fails to recognize his responsibility in one area and takes it on the chin in another as a consequence. He loses twice and, if not careful, will lose a third time when he vents his emotions on his wife, whom he is charged to protect emotionally!

It is also easy to see how satan can compound and increase sin, once given a place to stand.

Similar examples abound and add other complexities. One is maintenence of the home. Leaky faucets, toilets, roofs and electrical problems are usually initially detected by the wife and reported to the husband. He frequently has another agenda (What?! Does TV or golf have lower priority?) and is maddeningly slow to undertake correction. If the wife nags, things degenerate and the husband stops hearing or talking. If she takes matters into her own hands and calls the plumber, there are further complications in the wife's usurping "headship" as well as the potential economic loss and the deferral of the husband's lessons regarding his responsibilities. *God will teach him much faster if the wife trusts God to do so and does not interfere.* (A whole textbook could be written for wives on this. There is much good counsel already published regarding how wives can cooperate with God in letting Him work directly with their husbands without their manipulations or interference.)

Another example with yet other complications is in the disciplining of children. Mothers are not designed for direct confrontation with their teenage children. They are primarily their source of nourishment and mercy. Ultimately, by the time the children are teenagers, the husband must be an effective disciplinarian to whom the mother naturally (easily, routinely) refers problems which she experiences. ("The rod and reproof give wisdom, but a child who gets his own way brings shame to his mother," Prov. 29:15). Children should see that they cannot drive a wedge between Mother and her shield. Fathers are designed to keep Mother from being abused. Nothing will anger a normal father more quickly than seeing his children fail to honor their mother's position in the home (especially if they are copying their father's forms of abuse).

There is another side of this coin, also. Men create complications when they attempt to operate in areas for which their wives were designed to minister to the family, generally much more effectively than the men. Some husbands insist on having the final authority concerning furniture arrangements, interior decor, clothing, diet and many items associated with the management of the household for which God gave him his wife. He should delegate these matters to her, keeping in mind that she is the queen of the household. It is her throne and she is the keeper of the nest.

Following are some true examples of situations where men have broken down as their wives' shields in one or more of their three primary areas of responsibility.

In case 1, "Mac" was a married father who would not work unless he could find exactly what was suited to him. He felt that God wanted him to be a salesman and that other forms of work were demeaning and beneath him. He consequently spent quite a bit of time unemployed and his wife went to work. The economic hardship resulted in increasing debt, loss of adequate housing and family separations. The situation was further complicated because Mac's mother would frequently feed and house him, even when he was refusing to work and was failing to feed and house his family. His wife became exposed to destructive influences which she could not resist and became involved in an extra-marital affair. She sued for divorce and married the other man.

This story illustrates an important point. A man's primary fulfillment in work is in his providing economic strength for his family, not in the work itself. If he finds work which is fulfilling and satisfying, that is a plus. Praise the Lord for it! But he can be a successful man if he works at a job he does not greatly enjoy and still provides an economically secure "nest" within which he and his wife can share their relationship and raise their children. The world is filled with such men who spend their entire lives working at unpleasant, unfulfilling work and do so faithfully for the sake of their families. At the end of their lives, such men can have fulfillment knowing their life was expended in right priorities and that they have passed the good seed of their example onto their children.

Case 2 involves a man who became enmeshed in an extra-marital affair. His story is particularly interesting because he received Christ as Savior right at that time and began to rationalize about how he was going to help his girlfriend, who had just contracted cancer, by marrying her as soon as she could divorce her husband! He had commenced also to divorce his wife. In counselling, however, he became convicted that his girlfriend could never be healed by his usurping her husband's place in her life, and that he had failed as a husband in failing to provide his wife with physical, economic and emotional security. He contacted her to initiate reconciliation and discovered that the very previous evening she had been assaulted, badly beaten and robbed! This amplified his conviction and further motivated his steps toward reconciliation.

Case 3 illustrates several problems. A very successful sporting goods salesman was divorcing his wife because she could not control her spending. He made around $120,000 per year and she spent it all. In addition, she held a job in which she earned $5,000 per year and spent all that, too. Can the reader discern what this problem illustrates? Further questioning of the salesman confirmed that he was, indeed, the source of extreme emotional abuse of his wife. He was continuously running her down in every area of her life, accusing her of being a failure as a woman. Her job and spending rates indicated that she was both unfulfilled and insecure and sought by working outside the home and procuring material things to satisfy both needs. The man eventually came under conviction that he was the cause of his wife's failure to find fulfillment as a woman because of his emotional abuse.

There are many men who are successful economically and have also protected their wives from any physical abuse or danger, but who regularly assault them verbally. Instead of "shields," they become "sewer pipes" through which the destructive arrows of satan are fed directly to their wives. They vent their anger on their wives in a fashion that goes beyond the sharing of frustration and disappointments to the destruction of their wives' self-esteem. They do this to their own ultimate loss. "For no one ever hated his own flesh, but nourishes and cherishes it, just as Christ also does the church" (Eph. 5:29). When a breast is battered and bruised beyond a certain point, it will stop providing milk.

These situations do not arise out of nowhere. There are many inherited characteristics of both husbands and wives which spawn these situations. The curse of the law of generations assures that God will "visit the iniquity of the father on the children, and on the third and the fourth generations" of those who hate Him (Ex. 20:5, Deut. 5:9). But the blood of Jesus will destroy the curse when applied to any recognized and repented characteristic which has been handed down (Rom. 6:14, Eph. 1:7, Gal. 3:13).

Mac had lost his father years before and he was raised by his mother, who never led her son into the development of economic strength. He never got off her breast, so to speak, as he grew up. Consequently, he married without an inherent capability to work for the economic security of his family. There were also psychological problems which had to be worked through over an extended period with close brothers in the body of Christ. With strong support from the body of Christ and through the blood of Christ placed upon the curses he had inherited, he became stronger economically and able to minister to others.

In the third case, the insecure wife was a product of a broken home, and had inherited her insecurity from the manner in which her father used to treat her mother. For her, marriage was an escape into which she took all of her unresolved problems of insecurity. Still, her husband (and any other husband) has the capacity in Christ to heal her and deliver her to fulfilled womanhood, when he becomes her supporter and shield rather than a willing foil for the enemy to continue his efforts to destroy her.

When confronted by an inherited trait resulting from the "law of generations," husband and wife should pray together, repenting of their behavior and placing the blood of Jesus on the root and fruit of their sin which the curse has spawned, claiming freedom from the curse (Rom. 6:14) and cancelling its power to be passed on to their children. The blood of Jesus has this power. "For sin shall not be master over us, for we are not under law, but under grace" (Rom. 6:14).

An especially exciting opportunity for the husband and wife to act as a team and observe the supernatural work of God occurs when it is recognized that the husband is unable to carry out a job for which he is best suited and the wife is going to have to do it in his place. Using the car example again, it is not uncommon that situations occur where the husband cannot take the car in to the shop. What does the couple do? In the same manner that God can and will compensate with gifts in His children to minister to the whole body (1 Cor. 12), it is possible for the husband and wife to agree together in prayer regarding the dangers involved and for the husband to anoint his wife with the spirit of accountability to deal with the problem of ministering effectively to the family. God will go with her and perform miracles.

Christ does this regularly and permanently with believers who lose their spouses through death (giving men the gift of mercy and women that of accountability, meaning that they become capable of administering these gifts to their families when the spouse has died.)

Hence, the husband and wife should pray together, with the husband bestowing upon his wife his blessing and the power to administer accountability with discernment, wisdom and strength when she is confronted with decisions to be made at the garage, or in any other situation in which she may be have to represent the husband to obtain just service.

The same is true in reverse in situations in which (God forbid!) the husband has to stand in for the wife in matters of health and feeding of the family, maintaining the vitality of the home and meeting the needs of the children in her absence. She has the authority to anoint and place on him, in the name of Jesus, all of her capacity to minister these gifts. (It runs counter to the natures of most men to admit they have such obvious shortcomings in these areas, because they must then humble themselves to try to duplicate their wives' efforts. Most would rather give up and get sick or go to MacDonald's to feed the kids. But miracles lay just around the corner when we humble ourselves!)

The home is the model of the Church and all related levels of ministry. Our capacity to minister is developed in the home, where God's tools are sharpest and the heat is the greatest. If we cannot learn our lessons there, spurred on by love and the pain of failure, there is little hope for development of these capacities outside the home, where such incentives are lacking. If a man cannot submit to the demands of loving his wife and striving for her success, he will be of little help in praying and fasting for the success of anyone else in the Church! But through time, as he works diligently at his family tasks, he will develop increased capacity for ministry to other members of the body of Christ. Similarly, those who are unmarried who apply their gifts for the "work of service" (Eph. 4:11-13) before marriage will carry these capacities into marriage, to the blessing of their spouse and children and the work of God's Kingdom.

Work diligently at your tasks. Be faithful and patient in your trials. God intends to increase our capacities to minister to others until we become as Christ, whose capacity is limitless. Faithfulness to your tasks will enable God to supernaturally increase your time, your resources (finances, support, people to whom tasks can be delegated, etc.), your vision, and your power to hear the Father and minister His gifts according to His will! May this be your prayer and mine. Amen!

7

Loss of Manhood

*Should your springs be dispersed abroad, streams
of water in the street?*

Proverbs 5:16-17

The discussion of the previous chapter is only an introduction to the most devastating area of failure of the shield. This most serious failure of the shield, loss of manhood, causes destruction of families and the multiplication of bad seed that will destroy yet generations more.

Evidence is overwhelming that our nation's manhood is evaporating before our very eyes. Wholesale destruction of families, a 50% divorce rate, complete with nearly 90% of our women being thrust into the workplace; the myriads of children being raised in broken homes, lacking either a mother or father; spirits of sexual perversion running rampant; all of this testifies to the emasculation of American men. *Emasculation* means "loss of manhood." It is the inescapable consequence of sexual immorality.

Sexual immorality is the most devastating and destructive cause of ruin to a man. It destroys his capacity to do what he was designed by God to do. It destroys his manhood by violating the intended purposes for which he was given strength and headship over a woman and dissipates it by pouring it out upon the ground as "streams of water in the street." Many women become willing conspirators to this sin, believing the lie that they are somehow enhancing and satisfying their lover's needs and working to win his heart, unaware that they are actually destroying him and themselves as well. Without adequate protection and not designed to resist, they foolishly yield and become parties to their own destruction, although their spirits tell them they are in error.

A man's major life function is to provide protection for the woman God has for him and to yield his life in order to do it. This is essential if he is to reproduce his seed — the very essence of manhood. He has in him the capacity to do this, if he does not throw it away. However, when he has sexual intercourse with a woman outside of the marriage covenant, he violates his purpose in life in fundamental ways. He violates the woman physically and emotionally. He exposes her to the spirit of lust. He exposes her body to pregnancy and her mind to the fear of pregnancy. He perverts and shatters her God-given vision for fulfillment with a man who is committed to her well-being. If she is a virgin, he destroys her hymen and bonds her to him in her shedding of blood, physically and emotionally, for life (see Chapter Ten, "Bonding of Men and Women"). She was not designed to be given to more than one man. If she was not a virgin, he extends the power of the spirit of harlotry in her and partakes of that spirit himself. Since he violates God's command to use his manhood to the safe-keeping of his wife and seed, God removes his manhood from him. It dies in the same manner Adam died. It is lawfully handed over to the destroyer, according to the curse of the law.

Proverbs chapter five reveals the manner in which sexual immorality (fornication and adultery) destroys the man. Speaking of adultery (there is little distinction between this and fornication; we were designed to be faithful to one person both before and after marriage), God warns of how easily deceived a foolish young man is, and that he does not know that sexual sin leads him to death (Prov. 5:1-5, 22-23). Listen to His words describing what happens to the substance of the man if he fails to heed God's warning: "...do not go near the door of her house, lest *you give your vigor to others, and your years to the cruel one; lest strangers be filled with your strength, and your hard-earned goods go to the house of an alien.*" What is a man's vigor? What is his strength? These refer to his capacity to give life; his virility, his earning power, his physical and emotional capacity to maintain effective protection over his wife and their offspring. "His hard-earned goods" refers to material and economic strength for his family. These things are the capacity of manhood; i.e., his ability to provide for a successful, fulfilled wife and to raise up godly seed!

It is also suggested that the immoral man's life is either shortened or tormented, since his years are "given to the cruel one." Every category of manhood's capacity that we have identified is directly dissipated by sexual immorality!

We should take careful note of another significant point made in Proverbs chapter five: The foolish man will come to his senses after it is too late. This reveals an important truth. God is not intimidated by destruction. In fact, this chapter of Proverbs is strong testimony that God's primary agenda is that we "know the truth" and, as in the case of the prodigal son, God is quite willing for us to experience destruction in order to come to a knowledge of the truth. However, in the case of sexual immorality, it appears we are looking at dim prospects for being restored merely by coming to our senses (as was the prodigal son). "[When] you groan at your latter end, when your flesh and your body are consumed; and you say, 'How I have hated instruction! And my heart spurned reproof! And I have not listened to the voice of my teachers, nor inclined my ear to my instructors! I was almost in utter ruin in the midst of the assembly and congregation'" (Prov. 5:11-14). How much better to listen to instruction before folly brings destruction.

The alternative is God's positive admonition regarding sexual relationships. "Drink water from your own cistern, and fresh water from your own well. Should your springs be dispered abroad, streams of water in the streets? Let them be yours alone, and not for strangers with you. Let your fountain be blessed, and rejoice in the wife of your youth. As a loving hind and a graceful doe, let her breasts satisfy you at all times; be exhilarated always with her love. For why should you, my son, be exhilarated with an adulteress, and embrace the bosom of a foreigner?" (Prov. 5:15-20)

Consider what is meant by "springs" and "streams of water" in verse 16. These words describe what issues from the man and the question is whether he is going to limit this issue to his wife alone, or it be "wasted in the streets." The terms specifically refer to his sperm, his seed, his life-giving reproductive power, the very essence of his manhood and power to reproduce it. If he dissipates this, every other supporting aspect of his manhood will follow in dissipation.

The wife, in turn, is to be his only cistern, his drinking source, not to be shared with anyone. Her life-giving function of nourishment is well portrayed: "Let her breasts satisfy you at all times." She is to be his life-giving breast and he is to be hers and hers alone!

What about a man who commences sexual immorality with his girlfriend and later marries her? Isn't that all right? Doesn't it prove that they were really "married all along" in God's sight? Doesn't that prove that the man really loves his wife and that everything is all right as long as the two really love each other?

No, it does not!

Premarital sex is the single greatest cause of the destruction of marriages, because all of the factors we described above are at work in even *more* devastating and lasting ways. Furthermore, this sin ensures that the curse will be passed along by reproducing the seed of the parents in the children (Ex. 20:5, Deut. 5:9).

Here is what happens when a man and woman are involved in sexual immorality that may lead to marriage:

(1) The woman knows deep in her heart, by the life statement of the man (i.e., his actions, which speak louder than words), that his sexual gratification is more important to him than is his being an effective shield of protection over her. This knowledge shapes everything that she does later in response to him. Nothing he can ever say with words will change what she already knows in her heart. Her vital quest for a "knight in shining armor" who will protect and deliver her from evil, whom she has been seeking most of her life, is dashed, and she is faced with compromise.

(2) Guilt enters the picture and both the man and the woman seek to get rid of the guilt. Few find God's solution (at least immediately), which is to repent of it as sin and obtain forgiveness and healing through the blood of the Lord Jesus Christ. Instead they usually vainly attempt to make it "not sin." The most usual way is by alleging that premarital sex is "all right because we love each other." But things are not all right, nor are they equal between the man and woman. Because of their different designs, the woman needs to *receive* the security of the man's assurance and it is the man, as the shield, who must *provide* that assurance. Hence, he denies guilt, both to spare her and to justify his actions. He is now trapped in a perverted definition of "love."

(3) Both the man and the woman become involved in the bondage of expectations, the man in trying to prove that he truly loves the girl, and the girl in continually needing assurance that the man does indeed love her. This is the only way that the lie that "premarital sex is all right" can be sustained. The natural leading of this is into marriage. But this is not the end; it is only the beginning. The man will continue to try to prove his love for the woman for the rest of his life, and she will live the rest of her life in insecurity, seeking such assurance. Any time the man does something to show he loves the woman, he will receive no gratification or appreciation from his wife, because this is merely what she needs and expects. It is not exchanged on the basis of love freely given, the way God intended it to be.

(4) The woman knows the character of her husband cannot be trusted. She will not trust him with other women. Nor, as a proven untrustworthy basis of her security, can she freely submit to trust him for her welfare. She will tend strongly to provide for her own security. Even if they come into a life-changing

relationship with Christ and ministry later in life, these roots will greatly impact the effectiveness of their model of the husband-wife relationship and their ability to minister together, especially with women.

(5) Lacking security, the woman will not be able to find gratification in pouring out her life for her husband as she should. She will tend to look to her children or other sources of activity for her gratification.

(6) The woman becomes the head of the family in lieu of the man. This is true not only because the manhood of the man has been damaged, but *because conspiracy to sin always perverts the proper relationships intended by God.* We see this in a number of illustrations in the Bible, not all of them involving sexual sin.

a. *Samson and Delilah:* Samson, who rebelled against the counsel of his parents, pursued relationships with a series of ungodly women, driven by sensual lusts ("She looks good to me"). His first wife demonstrated her ascendency over him by enticing him to tell her the secret of his riddle to the Philistines. As a result of this fatal weakness, he paid a heavy economic penalty and his wife was given over to be defiled by another man who had been his friend (see Judges 14). After a recorded incident of harlotry, he came into an affair with Delilah. In the same manner as the previous woman, Delilah became ascendent over Sampson and manipulated him into revealing the secret of his strength to her, even though he had every reason to know that it would mean his destruction. She manipulated him in the name of his "proving that he loved her," and it resulted in his death. The root of Samson's weakness was in his sexual immorality and the ascendency of the women in his life over him as a result.

b. *David and Bathsheba:* David committed adultery with Bathsheba and as a result she became ascendent over David the rest of their lives. She was able to obtain an early promise from him that their son Solomon (not born as a result of the adultery, but thereafter) would become king after David. Many years later, when David lay on his death bed, she was able to make this promise stick and assure Solomon's ascension to the throne, though Solomon was not the eldest (2 Sam. 11,12; 1 Kin. 1, 2:22). (Note: Solomon was beloved by God and used by God as the wisest king Israel ever had. The point here is the role Bathsheba had in bringing it about.)

c. *David and Joab:* Joab was the commander of Israel's armies who conspired with David to put Uriah, Bathsheba's husband, to death. Joab came into ascendency over David and was a plague over David the rest of his life. He consistently manipulated and disobeyed David, even killing the king's son Absolom against his explicit orders. David was so powerless against Joab that he had to solve the problem by telling his son Solomon to kill Joab after he died (2 Sam. 11, 12; 2 Kin. 2:5-6).

d. *David and Jonathan:* This example is slightly more subtle. David and Jonathan walked a close walk as brothers, but this relationship came apart as a result of their conspiracy to lie to Jonathan's father, King Saul. In First Samuel chapter 19 it is recorded that Jonathan had a relationship with his father so sound that he was able to turn his father away from killing David by appealing to him with a proper appeal. He reminded Saul that it would be sin for the king to kill somone who had done him no harm (1 Sam. 19:5). The power of this appeal was so strong that it caused Saul to come to repentence and restore David to fellowship. Yet, in the next chapter, David manipulated Jonathan to agree to lie to Saul. Saul, being a father, discerned the lie right away. As a result, the relationship between Saul and Jonathan was seriously damaged and the relationship between Jonathan and David was permanently broken (1 Sam. 19:1-7; 1 Sam. 20).

We see that conspiracy to sin perverts or disrupts the godly relationship that God intends. In the case of the husband-wife relationship, pre-marital sex causes the woman to become the "head" of the family, unable to submit to the husband, unable to trust in God through the husband to provide for her essential needs of security because of the sin between them and the character defect that she knows to exist in her husband. The man, because of his loss of manhood, has neither the wisdom nor the power to recover his proper position.

(7) Finally, the woman, who is now the head of the family and finds her chief gratification, not in being the fulfilling fountainhead of her husband's success, but in other things such as her children or activities outside the home (and outside the protection of the husband), also finds no gratification in nourishing her husband and receiving his life in sexual union. The essential aspect of sexual union, being a fulfillment of the marriage covenant, has been robbed and turns to dust. She will become cold and lose interest in sex with her husband.

(8) The likely end result will be divorce and the assurance that the same defilement and destruction of fulfillment will be

passed on to their children. Of marriages that end in divorce today (50% of the total in the United States), 95% of couples were involved in premarital sex. What a sentence to pass on to your children! What a price to pay for satisfying the lusts of the flesh! What a price for failure to heed instruction and walking in folly!

What can we do? The situation would be hopeless were it not for the blood of Jesus! But Christ's blood is powerful for the removal of the curse in every sin for which there is repentance. In Jesus, we have forgiveness for our sin and destruction of the power of sin. For every man who has discarded his manhood in the lusts of deceit (Eph. 4:22), there is the potential for repentance and restoration in Christ. We have the propitiation of our sins (Rom. 3:25, 1 John. 2:2, 4:10) in the blood of Christ, our kind and merciful Lord and Savior. He is eager and able to work all things for our good, able to restore what the locusts have eaten (Joel 2:24-25) to the glory of God the Father! Hallelujah! Let no man despair. Jesus has come to set the captives free, that they may be free indeed to enjoy life abundantly.

Let every man who desires drink of the cup of Jesus, whose blood was given as the "blood of the new covenant, for the remission of sins," and let him place that blood on his sexual immorality through prayer, taking full responsibility for the damage he has done his wife and family. "Therefore, confess your sins to one another, and pray for one another, so that you may be healed" (James 5:16).

Dear Jesus, I confess and repent of my sexual immorality. I grieve that I have caused my wife's disappointment and loss of real happiness due to my failures as a man. Please restore me with Your blood. Please dissolve the effects of the curse of my sin on my family. Deliver me, please, into a place of righteousness in You, where I can be a true man of God and yield up my life in order to bring my wife into a place of fulfillment as a woman. Lord, help me to bring her into a place such as that to which Boaz brought Ruth. Let her find true gratification as a woman, to the glory of God, and show me how I may do that for her. Please deliver my children from the curse of the law of generations and help us together to deliver them to godly marriages in which they remain free of sexual immorality. Thank You for bringing me to this place. Make an honest man of me and bring these things to pass in my life no matter what the cost. Thank You, Lord. In Jesus' Name, Amen.

"If we confess our sins, He is faithful and righteous to forgive us our sins and to cleanse us from all unrighteousness" (1 John 1:9).

No more let sins and sorrows grow,
Nor thorns infest the ground;
He comes to make His blessings flow
Far as the curse is found,
Far as the curse if found,
Far as, far as the curse is found!

(3rd verse of "Joy to the World"
Words by Isaac Watts — 1719)

8

Restoration of Manhood: A Study of Judah, Part I

She is more righteous than I, inasmuch as I did not give her to my son Shelah.

Genesis 38:26

Judah came from a troubled family. His father Jacob had been a usurper and sown much bad seed, which passed onto his sons according to the law of generations (Ex. 20:5, Deut. 5:9). The three eldest sons were removed from their birthright of inheritance. Judah was fourth in line and was in as bad or worse shape than the rest.

He took his inheritance and made things even worse.

We can better appreciate the extent of the destruction which had entered Judah by first taking a closer look at his father Jacob and his three elder brothers.

After extorting (cheating) his brother Esau out of his birthright, Jacob fled to Haran, the land of his grandfather's and mother's brothers. There he produced a large family by four different women. He was in turn cheated and extorted at length by his father-in-law. Continuing to reap and sow the seeds of deception and broken relationships, Jacob had six sons by a woman he did not love and four by maid-servants before he had Joseph and Benjamin by Rachel, his first love and the one to whom he had bonded himself with fourteen years of work. Rachel died during the birth of Benjamin, his last son, thus making Benjamin the most precious of all his offspring.

Some other facets of Jacob's character are revealed in the fact that his wife Rachel stole her father Laban's idols when Jacob departed from Haran to return to Canaan (31:19). This suggests that Jacob had not taught or effectively witnessed to his most beloved of the God of his fathers Abraham and Isaac. Neither had he lived his life in such a fashion as to give her security apart from her father's idols. The primary concern of both Leah and Rachel upon his departure from Laban was over whether they still had any inheritance with their father Laban and the degree of amassed wealth that Jacob had accumulated. This is a mark of severe insecurity in Jacob's wives.

His mountain-top experience in wrestling with the angel was a turning point in his life. This produced the grace he received when he finally refused to hide behind but "passed on ahead" of his family to face his brother Esau (whom he had deceived and who easily could have killed him). But it did not produce any significant life changes in Jacob for the moment. He remained a fearful and powerless man.

His weakness in serving as a shield is also demonstrated in the ill-fated visit of his daughter Dinah to "visit the daughters of the land" (Gen. 34). In her naivete and lack of protection from her father, she was raped by a local prince. That in turn was marked by a bloodbath of the local inhabitants at the hands of Jacob's sons, led by Simeon and Levi (the second and third sons), whom Jacob could not control and who took things into their own hands. Their vicious retribution against an entire city reflected their father's impotence and exactly portrayed the depths of deception which had characterized his life. The best rebuke he could muster afterward was a self-pitying cry that now he had become "odious among the inhabitants of the land" and that they now would probably attack and destroy him.

Despite his earlier victory with the angel and in facing his brother Esau, Jacob had not rid himself of the foreign idols in his family. It was only after God again told him to move on to Bethel that he appears to have made a sincere turn toward God that prompted him to cease tolerating foreign idols (Gen. 35:2). However, by this time the power of the curse was heavy upon his sons.

Jacob's sons were living with the legacy of the seeds he had sown. His inability to raise up his sons in proper discipline and without partiality resulted in hatred and jealousy between Joseph and Jacob's other sons. Their lack of discipline and godly fear of their father caused them to sell Joseph into slavery and lie to their father, telling him that Joseph had been killed.

It is noteworthy that the first-born son, Reuben, showed here some inherited sense of his responsibility for his younger brother Joseph, inasmuch as he attempted to intercede for his life. But, it was actually Judah who later talked the others out of killing Joseph and persuaded them to sell him to the Egyptians. It is significant also that Reuben, infected by his father's loss of manhood, had earlier committed sexual immorality with Bilhah, one of his father's concubines. He thereby lost both his birthright (Gen. 49:4) and the sufficiency of manhood to save his brother Joseph.

But what honor is there among thieves, or what righteousness is there among the perverted and depraved? Judah, himself raised in this environment, was emasculated as well, and after Joseph was sold into slavery, it is recorded that he was also involved in sexual immorality.

Chapter 38 of Genesis records the fact that Judah bore three sons by a Canaanite woman and took a wife, Tamar, for the first son, Er. Because Er was evil in the sight of the Lord, He took his life (Gen. 38:6,7). According to what was to become the law, Judah gave Tamar to his second son, commanding him, "Go in to your brother's wife, and perform your duty as a brother-in-law to her, and raise up offspring for your brother." But the second son knew that the offspring would not be his, so "he wasted his seed on the ground, in order not to give offspring to his brother. But what he did was displeasing to the Lord; so He took his life also" (Gen. 38:8-10).

At this point Judah became concerned that his third son might die, as his brothers had, so he put Tamar off and sent her to her father's house, arranging to wait until his son Shelah grew up. He never intended to keep his word (Gen. 38:11).

Judah therefore became involved in the obstruction of the reproduction of his own seed through lack of faith and efforts to preserve his offspring through his own devices.

When it became evident that Judah was not going to give her as a wife to his youngest son, Tamar took things into her own hands by disguising herself as a prostitute and successfully enticing Judah to have sexual intercourse with her (Gen. 38:12-19). More deceit. More sexual immorality. But in the ensuing events a revealing thing happened.

When Judah discovered that his daughter-in-law Tamar was pregnant, he ordered her to be brought out and burned. But she had wisely secured his signet ring, cord and staff as tokens of his pledge of payment for the prostitution, and she presented them as proof that it was Judah who had fathered her child. Judah was exposed in his immorality and hypocrisy!

What was also exposed was that Judah had a heart that could be convicted of sin.

When Judah was confronted with his signet ring, cords and staff, his response was immediate and it was not primarily focused on his harlotry. He responded, "She is more righteous than I, inasmuch as I did not give her to my son Shelah." In this response we see that Judah, despite his depravity, was able to see the underlying, root sin of which he was convicted: He had denied his son to Tamar. Perhaps he was convicted of his disobedience and unbelief. Or perhaps this was a more fundamental breach of righteousness according to the standards of his time than his having lain with a prostitute. But in this quick repentance and sensitivity Judah revealed the nature of his heart, which is what God looks upon in His choice of a man to do His work (1 Sam 13:14, 16:7).

We see in this the basis of God's later choice of Judah as the one through whom He would later bear the true Seed of manhood and whose heart would be reproduced in David.

But God had considerably more work to do. Judah had yet to go through the fiery ordeal that would make a man of him.

9

Restoration of Manhood:
A Study of Judah, Part II

Now, therefore, please let your servant remain instead of the lad
a slave to my lord, and let the lad go up with his brothers.
Genesis 44:33

Throughout the years that Judah and his brothers had to meditate on their crime against their brother, interesting things were taking place in Joseph's life. God was making him into a pattern of the Messiah, the Lord Jesus Christ. Raised as a shepherd, rejected and betrayed by his brothers, sold for a few pieces of silver and given up for dead by his father, he became a king over the land with absolute authority, second only to Pharaoh himself. He became an instrument of righteousness in forging a new man of Judah.

Prior to Joseph's sale into captivity we see no reference to God in the discussion of Jacob's sons, and no evidence of their awareness of Him in the affairs of their lives. This is another legacy of the seeds sown by their father. Coupled with his inability to pass manhood to his sons, Jacob was unable to pass a fear of God on to them. As they perceived their father, so they perceived God.

Hence, in order to change their perceptions, it was necessary that they be brought to accountability under another stronger and more righteous authority.

Joseph was somehow (perhaps through dreams) given a knowledge of God with which to face his life as a captive and lived a life of high accountability from the age of 17 onward, as a slave. Separated at an early age from his depraved brothers and placed in a crucible, he was given the opportunity to be shaped into a righteous man and God did the necessary work. Having been forged, he became qualified to be used as an instrument in the forging of others.

The chief gift he received was that of discernment; discerning what God was doing and what he needed to do to work in harmony with God. He rose in favor and came before Pharaoh.

Joseph was given the discernment with which to advise Pharaoh of the coming years of famine and how to prepare for it. He was given administration of the kingdom. Eventually, the famine came (Gen. 41) and his brothers showed up in Egypt to buy grain (Gen. 42:1-7).

Can anyone comprehend the discernment that Joseph must have had to have heard the voice of God and be used to convict his brothers of sin? Was he unconscious of his approach, or did he first develop a plan (see Prov. 16:9)? The Scriptures give us little insight into that question, but offer great insight regarding God's basic precepts.

The chief work that Joseph did in his brothers was to build a fear of God into them. All knowledge and wisdom starts with the fear of God (Prov. 1:7). He lavished favor on them while keeping them in a strong environment of accountability. He thereby worked in harmony with God to enable Him to build into them this godly fear. Most of the work was done by the Spirit of God.

Joseph did not tell his brothers what he was doing (pearls before swine? See Matthew 7:6), and he did at least one thing which might reasonably be thought of as deceptive. Let us take a closer look. From Genesis chapter 42, and the initial circumstances of his brothers' arrival, when Joseph recognized them but they did not recognize him (vs.1-8), we see the following:

(1) Joseph took his initial cue from the dreams God had given him: He was to serve the role of authority in which God had placed him and make his brothers bow down to him (vs. 9). He put immediate pressure on them, as foreigners, in the way that seemed most obvious, testing their motives by accusing them of being spies.

(2) He considered the information that they initially provided him in response, in which it was evident that Benjamin was precious to his father and that they were living a lie regarding Joseph's alleged death (vs. 13).

(3) He determined to test them in a way that would make them accountable not only to him, but also to their father Jacob (vs. 15-20).

The Spirit of God commenced work in Joseph's brothers immediately, and they saw at once the relationship between the distress they were in and that of Joseph's soul that had been on him when he pleaded in vain with his brothers years before (vs. 21). Reuben, the first-born, still failed to take any part of their sin onto himself, blaming his brothers for failing to listen to him and decrying their actions as sin.

Joseph understood their conversation and wept in secret, then bound and emprisoned Simeon, the second born (possibly attempting to enable God to continue to work with Reuben, the first-born). Unknown to his brothers, he paid for their grain, placing their money back in their grain sacks (giving to them generously in secret, probably having no ulterior motive). Immediately the conviction of God in their lives progressed further and they began to mention Him by name in awe and fear (vs. 22-28) .

When they returned home and the matter was placed before Jacob, Reuben was again ineffectual as the first-born, although he attempted to play his role in exhorting his father to action. However, he fell short, seeing no better option than to offer up his two sons in sacrifice if he is unsuccessful in bringing Benjamin home; he still did not comprehend that he could offer up himself. He was still in the bondage of failing to recognize and repent from his own sin. His offer had no power and Jacob kept his sons at home (vs. 29-38) .

Chapter 43 brings Jacob's family to the inevitable; they again run out of grain. We see Jacob as his normal emasculated, ineffectual self; he is whimpering in self-pity as he blames his sons for treating *him* badly by having revealed that they had another brother (Gen. 43:6). But now he has approached the opportunity for grace. He has neared the point at which that he realizes he must act.

Judah, the son who once came to repentence for his sins, now steps forward. He speaks the message given them by the man in Egypt clearly, so there is no misunderstanding, no more wishful thinking. Then he says to his father, "Send the lad with me, and we will arise and go, that we may live and not die, we as well as you and our little ones" *[Note the scope of his concerns]*. I myself will be surety for him; you may hold me responsible for him. If I do not bring him back to you and set him before you, then let me bear the blame before you forever" (Gen. 43:8-9).

Hear the words of Jesus! Can anyone recognize the call of a son which the father cannot refuse? *"Let me take his place. I will bear the blame. I will restore him to you or bear the blame forever."* This is gap-standing. This is load-bearing. This is the example Moses would also follow 400 years later in the wilderness, when he interceded for sinful Israel, willing to have his name taken out of the Book of Life if God would not spare the people. God loves it. It is His measure of a man because it is His way and the measure of His Son, Jesus.

Jacob agreed to Judah's proposal and suddenly found new vitality. With his decision to allow Benjamin to go his mind cleared and he issued orders. "Take gifts... Take double the money back... And may God Almighty grant you compassion in the sight of the man, that he may release to you your other brother and Benjamin. And as for me, if I am bereaved of my children, I am bereaved" (Gen. 43:11-14).

What power there is in such a decision — "If I die, I die!" (Esth. 4:16)

Upon the return of the brothers to Egypt, Joseph held a luncheon banquet and wept at the sight of Benjamin, his brother. Then he again had all their money secretly placed in their grain sacks and, in addition, had his silver cup placed in Benjamin's. After they left, he gave his chief steward instructions to overtake them and recover the cup.

Imagine how relieved the brothers were after they had cleared the outskirts of the city! They had made good their escape! The prime minister of Egypt believed their innocence. Their secret was still safe. They had got Simeon out of prison! And Benjamin was safe! Judah was breathing a sigh of relief; their father would be pleased with them. Just then, Joseph's house steward came riding up behind them with bad news — they were accused of stealing Joseph's silver cup!

Could this really be a crisis? They were innocent, weren't they? They pledged the death of whoever was found among them having the cup. But one can almost hear the clap of doom resound in their spirits. One can hear their spirits witnessing to them, "The jig is up! The bloodguiltiness of our hands on our brother Joseph is upon us! Why is nature conspiring so to expose our sin? Why can't we escape it? This is God. Our sins are finding us out!"

They search the packs and find the cup in Benjamin's sack. Back they go in dismay to the city — to prison, to doom, to confrontation with the sin in their hearts.

Now they come to the moment of truth. Judah offers one more compromise, one more "knee jerk" of the natural man, implying that it is their corporate iniquity involved; "How can we justify ourselves? God has found out the iniquity of your servants; behold, we are my lord's slaves, both we and the one in whose possession the cup has been found" (Gen. 44:16).

But Joseph knows that this is a lie. Benjamin was not involved in Joseph's being sold into slavery; he is innocent. Joseph issues the coup de grace.

"Far be it from me to do this. The man in whose possession the cup has been found, he shall be my slave; but as for you, go up in peace to your father" (Gen. 44:17).

Now they are squarely confronted with their sin. It has been presented to them that they can escape if they repeat their first crime.

Why shouldn't they? Isn't Benjamin just as much a favorite with their father Jacob as their brother Joseph was? Can't they just explain to their whimpering father that Benjamin was caught as a thief and was kept a slave as a result? It wasn't their fault, was it? Isn't that the truth (as far as they know)? If they agree as a group, doesn't that give them the protection of being in the "mob" majority? This decision will return them to their wives and families.

But one man has the love of his father. He is ready to provide a life-giving response — his own life. He knows his father will die if his beloved son Benjamin is not returned to him. He approaches Joseph to speak to him privately. "Oh my lord, may your servant please speak a word in my lord's ears, and do not be angry with your servant; for you are equal to Pharaoh" (Gen. 44:18).

There Judah pours out his heart, expressing his father's grief over the loss of his first son and his love for his remaining son Benjamin, explaining that his father's "life is bound up in the lad's life." He is totally unaware that he is vividly expressing his own love for his father.

Then he says, "I have become surety for the lad to my father, saying, 'If I do not bring him back to you, then let me bear the blame before my father forever.' Now, therefore, please let your servant remain instead of the lad a slave to my lord, and let the lad go up with his brothers. For how shall I go up to my father if the lad is not with me, lest I see the evil that would overtake my father?" (Gen. 44:32-34)

Joseph could no longer control himself. This eloquent plea from one willing to stand in place of his brother, who had clearly repented and had come to love his father, broke Joseph's heart. Mercy abounded and his heart overflowed in tears.

Restoration of the entire family was accomplished, deliverance from hunger and from the bondage of many years. Reconciliation and forgiveness entered in. And one man became totally freed because he had come into the place of manhood and had offered himself up for the sake of his father and brother. His spirit, attitude and "seed" were altered. The future of history and pathway of regeneration in Christ Jesus were ordained as a result.

Later, when their father was on his deathbed, Jacob's (Israel's) sons heard his prophecy. The first three sons were rejected from their birthright, but these words were spoken over Judah:

Judah is a lion's whelp; From the prey, my son, you have gone up. He couches, he lies down as a lion, and as a lion, who dares rouse him up? The scepter shall not depart from Judah, nor the ruler's staff from between his feet, until Shiloh comes, and to him shall be the obedience of the peoples. He ties his foal to the vine, and his donkey's colt to the choice vine; he washes his garments in wine, and his robes in the blood of grapes. His eyes are dull from wine, and his teeth white from milk.

Genesis 49:9-12

This is Messianic prophecy. *Shiloh* is a Hebrew word for "peace" and the prophecy contains many of the symbols later recognized as signifying the Messiah: lion, obedience of the peoples (Isaiah), foal and donkey's foal (Zechariah), choice vine, wine and blood, and the bridegroom. The prophecy even includes the timing of the Messiah's appearing ("The scepter shall not depart ... until Shiloh comes...")

Judah's heart, easily repentant, was later reproduced in David. How did God do this?

Do you recall the questions raised at the conclusion of the chapter on Boaz, the man's man who walked in the ways necessary to bring Ruth into the place of fulfillment? Recall that we wondered why God saw fit for the writer of Ruth to place ten unusual generations of geneology at the very conclusion of the chapter, to wit:

Now these are the generations of Perez: to Perez was born Hezron, and to Hezron was born Ram, and to Ram, Amminadab, and to Amminadab was born Nahshon, and Nahshon, Salmon, and to Salmon was born Boaz, and to Boaz, Obed, and to Obed was born Jesse, and to Jesse, David.

Ruth 4:18-22

These generations are not even bounded on either end by the generation of Boaz and Ruth. Hence, the question again arises, why did God consider it important to highlight this?

We read in Deuteronomy the curse that was on Judah as a result of his iniquity. His abomination in sexual sin, his fornication with his daughter-in-law Tamar, produced two sons, one of which was Perez. Perez was of illegitimate birth, born of incest (Lev. 18:15).

Hear the word of the Mosaic Law regarding an illegitimate birth. "No one of illegitimate birth shall enter the assembly of the LORD; none of his descendants, even to the tenth generation, shall enter the assembly of the LORD" (Deut. 23:2). Now count the number of generations between Judah and David!

We see that God was working in two ways in the line of Judah to honor (to raise up so that we could "see") the precepts of manhood which He had built into Judah. First, He enabled the line of Judah to produce a man's man, Boaz, who could walk in the image of Christ with respect to women, thus enabling his blessing and bringing into fulfillment (and the lineage of Christ) a godly gentile woman, Ruth. Second, He enabled the repentent heart of the regenerated man, Judah, to be passed to the tenth generation of men to produce David, in whom were also placed the Messianic promises and the man "after God's own heart" (1 Sam. 13:14) who would walk again in the "assembly of the LORD."

God, who always does exceedingly abundantly, beyond anything that we ask or think (Eph. 3:20), did much more with David than to merely restore him to the inner assembly of fellowship with God. He gave to David a richness of fellowship that exceeded any other recorded up to that time among the sons of Abraham. He gave to him clearer promises than had yet been revealed pertaining to the promise of the coming Messiah, and a more concise picture of God's great character and personality (primarily through David's psalms). David also became one of the "prototypes" of a shepherd-king, pointing to the nature of Messiah, the very essence and character of true manhood.

The release of this blessing into David's life was tied to Judah, the man corrupted by sexual sin, steeped in the iniquity of a family of ineffectual men, who finally came under the conviction of God for his sin. Through considerable pain, God brought Judah to a point of "getting things right" in his priorities and making a right stand before God and men — ready to give up his life for the sake of those he loved.

Blessed be all those men who inherit these promises into their own hearts and in whom the Spirit of God rises to bring about conviction regarding the true purposes of their lives.

Dear God, please give us the manhood and the power to reproduce it in our sons. In Jesus' Name. Amen.

10

Bonding of Men and Women

Consequently they are no longer two, but one flesh.
What therefore God has joined together, let no man
separate.

Matthew 19:6

Countless are the women who would like to know a method by which they could bond the soul of a man to themselves. Nearly as countless are those who have tried and failed, destroying their prospects for a happy marriage and successful family as a result, by resorting to "what seems best to them." How few know that God has provided a means by which the man God has chosen to fulfill her dreams of happiness can be bonded to her for life.

In sorting out the errors that young women make in their pursuit of happiness, the first is probably in not recognizing that God has a righteous method for supporting and enabling their dream in the first place. They step outside of God's provision and "turn to their own way" (Is. 53:6). Once there, their own devices lead them into further error, the chief of which is failure to recognize that men and women are not bonded to each other in the same fashion. Many women succumb to the demands of the man and their temptation to satisfy him sexually, thinking that it will further secure his affections, only to find, to their consternation, that it does not accomplish the expected results. His soul remains unknit to hers, but hers is bound to him permanently. What an awful way to discover a universal truth!

Women are bonded to men through the first occasion of sexual intercourse, but the reverse is not true. Men, even men who are rapturously in love, are not bonded by sexual intercourse. God has another method for bonding a man to a woman; by passing him through fire on behalf of the woman. He must pay a ransom.

God gives special attention to the uniqueness of a woman's becoming bonded to a man through sexual intercourse in His provision under the Mosaic Law for a virgin seized and seduced by a man. "If a man finds a girl who is a virgin, who is not engaged, and seizes her and lies with her and they are discovered, then the man who lay with her shall give to the girl's father fifty shekels of silver, and she shall become his wife because he has violated her; he cannot divorce her all his days" (Deut. 22:28-29). This provision is distinct from those for harlotry or for the rape of a girl engaged to another man. In the latter case, if she is raped in the city and did not cry out, she is found guilty of harlotry and stoned along with the man. However, if she is raped in the country, it is assumed that she had no opportunity to cry out and only the man is stoned. This same regard for the innocence of a girl who has been wrongfully seduced but is "discovered" applies in God's prescription that the man become her husband. It is the only action which is compatible with her innocence and with the fact that in her heart she has become "bonded" to him for life.

The first man with whom a girl has sexual union will occupy her heart's emotions the rest of her life. She will desire to nourish him and enhance him in a fashion which occupies her creative thoughts and meditations. She will place the dreams of girlhood onto him and thereafter attach her fulfillment as a woman onto his life. Even if she is unable to marry him, she will dream of him and think of him while making love with the man whom she later marries. She will remain bonded to him as long as he lives unless this tie is broken in the name and by the blood of the Lord Jesus.

Men, on the other hand, do not carry or identify their life fulfillment in sexual union. This is in keeping with the fact that their major life function is in being a shield over the woman, not in enhancing her or nourishing her through sexual fulfillment. It is also unfortunately true that, by the time men have their first sexual union with a woman, they will have experienced orgasm scores or hundreds of times through dreams and masturbation. Hence, in one of the major areas in which sexual fulfillment is reached for the man, intercourse is not a new experience, as it is for the woman. For her, it is in her union and fulfillment of the man in which her own most intense experience takes place.

It is noted that some teach that both women and men are bonded through sex, citing the love between Shechem the son of Hamor and Dinah the daughter of Jacob, when Shechem raped her (Gen. 34). Without reading anything into the lines, however, it may be safe to say that since Shechem had just met her, he was primarily motivated in his subsequent actions by his brand new enraptured and romantic love for Dinah rather than sexual bonding and had only just commenced the things which would have truly bonded him to her at the time he and his family were slaughtered by Jacob's sons. In fact, it was his willingness to undergo circumcision on her behalf that proves that he did, indeed, love her and is a clue regarding what God has for men who are motivated by the love of a woman.

Also, as an illustration of something quite the opposite occurring, we have the incident of Amnon's rape of his step-sister Tamar. They knew each other quite well. There was no infatuation or romantic love, only Amnon's lust. Sexual intercourse with Tamar did not bond him to her at all. It only caused him to despise her, even though she had resisted him.

The dreams that girls carry of a "knight in shining armor" who will battle for them, win them and carry them off on a white horse are not nonsense. Nor are their dreams of complete and intimate union with a man who will be true to them and upon whom they can pour out their lives "happily ever after." God gives girls these dreams. The are the motivational vision He provides, the picture of the pathway toward life fulfillment He has authored for them. That is where God wants to take His beloved daughters for their joy and happiness. These visions also contain signposts, which all such visions contain, to alert their recipients to their actual features as they occur along the way.

What are the features of the girl's vision? First is her hero in the role of a warrior, a defender under whom she will be able to live securely. Second, he must pass a test, some kind of a trial of fire, in order to gain possession of her. It perhaps involves, figuratively, storming a castle in which she is held captive. Third, he successfully overcomes formidable obstacles (i.e., a dragon or the castle's defenses) in order to gain her. In so doing, he proves his love for her and wins her heart.

Praise the Lord! This is exactly what God has in mind. And fulfillment of this scenario is just as important for the man as it is for the girl. In fact, it is essential to the fulfillment of her security and happiness! This is the scenario of how the man becomes bonded to the woman!

It is God's intention to secure the bonding of the man to the girl *before the marriage covenant* through the trials he undergoes to win her, and to secure the bonding of the girl to the man *after the marriage covenant on the wedding bed.*

The castle he has to storm is properly the girl's father, God's chief authority in her life, who stands as her covering and protection until the boy has proved himself and responsibility is transferred. This is the trial by fire which a young man should properly undergo and needs to undergo if he is to come into manhood! A young woman has no idea of the clutter of childish foolishness that a "man" will carry into their marriage, working to its destruction, if he is not first given the opportunity to be forged and refined under her father's scrutiny. She cannot understand and was not designed to understand.

Fathers are God's agents for bonding men to their daughters. It is one of a daughter's first major areas of learning to trust God to work through authority. It will also shape her future relationship with her husband in the same area of enablement to trust God to work through him. Her overwhelming natural tendency is to jump down out of the castle and get on with the business of lathering up her hero with mercy and nourishment while he is still a little boy. (If she does, she will unfortunately leave him that way — a boy.) God's plan for her, instead, is to trust in Him to work through her father and to stay under his protective shield until he gets the job done.

Men are ultimately bonded to women according to the price they have to pay to gain their welfare and win their security. The more they pay, the greater the bonding. For a young man intent upon being the girl's security, this starts out first by having to "win" her. It is good for him (can you believe this, young ladies?) to have to work to win his sweetheart. For his own sake he needs to be accountable to someone who is older, wiser and, because of his position of righteous concern over her welfare, in an unassailable position of strength. The young man needs to come up against someone who knows him like a book, who knows how he thinks (or rather, does not think), how he behaves, and who can discern his motives at a glance. Fathers were designed to do this. Young men know this and will strive to avoid giving a girl's father a chance for any meaningful scrutiny.

But young men were also designed to find themselves exposed to risk and to overcome their fears, to be held accountable in their motives, purified in their behavior and in having the fog of distractions removed from their thoughts regarding what is really important in their lives. They must make some inner discoveries. They need to confront the risk of losing and make some hard decisions to persevere, to forge ahead regardless of the risks. It takes accountability to a higher power to accomplish this. By the time he speaks of marriage a man must have invested a price and know the truth in his heart. "This girl is worth the price! I'll pay it!" A man must have to "face the dragon" and "storm the castle" in order to know this truth. He who comes into marriage without it is robbed, missing the knowledge of the value of his bride based on the price he has paid. He remains a little boy.

If men don't learn this thoroughly before marriage, the next opportunity for them to consider values and alternatives will be when they consider the cost of a more effective marriage versus that of divorce. Bonding of the man's heart should be so powerful that the pain of divorce is more than he can seriously contemplate.

We gain in these principles an improved understanding of why Jacob did not bond to his first wife, Leah, and why she was so heartsick over his lack of love for her for so many years (Gen. 29:15-35). Imagine being bonded to a husband who does not love you! However, Jacob was bonded to Rachel even before marrying her because he worked seven years to win her hand. He had invested himself in her, not Leah! His bonding is evident in his willingness to work yet another seven years for Rachel, even after discovering he had been cheated! He gained Leah as his wife through duplicity; not that of Leah, but her father's. No matter; it was through duplicity. What was the result? Young ladies reading this should seriously consider the foundations they desire for their marriage, rejecting duplicity and seeking bonding according to God's plan.

Daughters, do you want to entrust to God the very best for your marriage? Then trust God to use your father as your chief agent for securing for you God's very best in a man and one who is already thoroughly bonded to you on your wedding night. If he can't face up to your father, then you don't want him!

There is another thing here that women need to keep in mind. A girl's attractiveness is greatly enhanced by the confident demonstration of her life-style that she is open and confidently submissive to her father, without any manipulative or untrusting tendencies to avoid his guidance or directions. Men desire to have a woman as their wife who is this way, who is not going to contest with them over the headship of the family nor subvert their leadership. They admire a girl who is confident under her father. They want that for themselves and may test a girl to see if it is genuine. A girl's attitude toward her father will speak to a man's spirit. If she reflects that she is comfortable in trusting in God to work through her father, then his own spirit will identify the fact that this is the attitude she will carry into marriage.

This attitude of a quiet and peaceful spirit under authority will make even an average-looking girl irresistibly beautiful to a man! He will take on a good-sized castle to secure that for himself (1 Pet. 3:1-6)!

God's perfect ideal for bonding between bride and bridegroom is presented in His model for the ages, Jesus and His Church. Jesus bonded with His bride at the foundation of the world when He resolved the price of salvation and embarked upon His plan. The marriage contract was consummated when He poured out His blood and had His body broken for her on Calvary. He has long been bonded to us. However, we were not yet bonded to Him.

How did we become bonded to Him? We received His seed. Each member of the bride has had a particular personal moment when we received the Word of Life. It penetrated our heart, even as the Holy Spirit worked life in the womb of the virgin Mary; "Be it done to me according to your word" (Luke 1:38). We received Him. His reproductive living seed was given a place in the womb of our heart. A woman's womb is only a picture of how we receive true life from the Living God and bonding to our Maker and Shield. When we received Him into our innermost, we bonded to Him. The marriage became consummated. He became our Husband, Lord and Savior forever.

11

Sovereignty: A Letter to Daughter

These words, which I am commanding you today, shall be on your heart;
and you shall teach them diligently to your [children]...
                                                    Deuteronomy 6:6-7

Dear Daughter,

I am hastening to give you some of the lore which every daughter should have in learning about how their dates, suitors, husbands and (later) sons think and operate. They are a creation of God just as you are, but with quite different functions built into their natures. They are fallen, besides, so opposing forces are working within them.

I mentioned to you in my earlier note that men behave contradictorily (just as women do, but in a different way). This is the way it operates.

When a man pursues a girl, obviously it is because he is attracted to her. What does he find attractive? On the surface it is her nourishment and uplifting of him — her power to contribute to his peace, joy and well-being (his view of himself, his health and motivations). But beyond this, ideally, and more than any other motivation, it is her purity. In young men who have not been involved in immorality, the mere suggestion that the girl is willing to be immoral with him or has had sex with other boys will be a complete turn-off. Once he has become involved (and possessed) with immorality, this changes and he is driven by mixed motivations which grow more and more perverted, depending upon how far down the pit of immorality he has gone. But underlying all his motivations to marry, nothing changes. He desires to have a companion who is pure and he desires to possess purity for himself. Men, the same as Christ, desire a bride who is "sanctified," that is, set apart for themselves alone. And few men have the capacity to truly wipe the past clean and to forgive (and forget the sins of) a woman who has been a harlot or immoral, the way Jesus has forgiven His bride.

Through all of his delight and the joy he has in giving himself up in pursuit of the girl, the man ultimately desires to gain sovereignty, because his function as a shield and head over the woman always works to cause him, by nature, to seek this position. He is inherently in the game of conquest, even though it might not immediately rear its head in sexual form. Hence, once he gets possession of any part of the girl (her time, travel, affections, phone calls, money, car, schedule, priorities, etc.) he will begin to rule over them. He will assert his desires in these areas in quite a different fashion than when he was pursuing her, *before* she had yielded these particulars to him.

If he doesn't get sovereignty, especially after he thinks he has gained it, or sometimes in an attempt to gain it, he will behave as a little boy and assert some kind of challenge, ultimatum or penalty on the girl because she has refused to submit.

At the same time, once affections are mutually exchanged, he begins on the inexorable road of seeking to gain the ultimate token of his sovereignty, the girl's body. It is in his nature to seek to gain this territory as a seal of his sovereignty over the woman. And that is exactly what it is. It is in his nature to seek it, with or without the covenant agreement which God has ordained for both the man and woman to commit their lives to each other.

Keep in mind that a woman's first sexual union binds her for life to the man. The reverse is not true, as I believe we have made clear. (The man's binding to the woman is related to the price he pays for winning her, saving her or working for her welfare.)

Also, since it is the woman's inherent nature to be submitted to a man in sovereignty over her, and to nourish him and satisfy his needs for well-being, it may be seen that the power he has to extort her sexual submission outside of the marriage covenant is great. The woman is not designed to resist this kind of pressure. That's why fathers were designed and ordained to be a protective covering over the daughter until the man has been (truly) won to her — until he has been *purified, purged, refined, stripped of much of his little boy foolishness, made transparent and accountable for his thoughts and motives, resolved in his mind that she is worth the laying down of his life.*

Also, in exactly the same fashion and for exactly the same reasons, it is not possible to withdraw any territory that has been given to the man without *extreme* repercussions. The nature of any territorial sovereignty is to "walk the territory," to review again its boundaries, to reassert the "feel" and identity of the lord over the land. (You can picture me walking my yard in Alexandria or Jefferson's daily ride at Monticello or the wild male animal daily restaking his territory with urine signs.) That is one reason it is so difficult to retreat from any level of immorality once it has been commenced. It is all familiar territory, which has once been gained (by the male) or given away (by the female).

If a man loves a girl and "succeeds" in gaining her sexually outside of marriage, he has actually failed in the greatest sense of the word in which a man can fail. His fallen nature has led him, in pursuit of sovereignty and self-gratification, into destroying the thing that was of most value to him, his girl's purity. Hence his manhood has failed and his capacity to work effectively as a man has been permanently destroyed. (Only the blood of Jesus can restore what the canker has destroyed and what the wild locusts have eaten.)

We have also talked about where his guilt will lead him in marriage and where the girl's resulting problems will lead her in the marriage as well — to the ultimate destruction of the marriage and the passing of their iniquity to the children.

Do not underestimate the power of purity. It is God's strongest weapon. It has brought many men to repentence and glory.

Also, do not overestimate your power to resist and to "see through" and handle all the spirits that work in the men you date. "Let him who thinks he stands take heed, lest he fall." You and I need to work cooperatively to assure that you are under a shield which works to refine the man you would marry and to assure his and your welfare and happiness. That is the way God designed it to work.

See you soon, honey.

I love you.

Dad

12

Fathers as Agents

*Fathers, do not provoke your children to
anger; but bring them up in the discipline
and instruction of the Lord.*

Ephesians 6:4

Girls become interested in boys at an early age, considerably before the reverse is true. Long before they enter into romantic relationships, they begin to form dreams and visions of the man they will marry and of what marriage will be like. Eventually, they get interested to the point of finding out more about boys. So they go to their mothers.

Now, does that make sense? Why should a girl go to her mother to find out about boys? What does her mother know? The only judgment we can place on her knowledge of men is the man she picked out for her daughter's father. Everyone knows how that turned out! Women really know very little about men.

The reason most girls go to their mothers to find out about boys is that their fathers drop out of the job God really created for them. Due to a variety of things, mainly ignorance and immaturity, they do not have a relationship with their daughters in which her efforts to inquire about her most urgent subject of interest can be supported. His own attitudes toward sex and romance probably being perverted also, if not at least immature, his natural reaction to her deepest levels of interest will tend to be judgmental and insensitive; she will close off further communication because she knows her father is opposed to her pursuit of this interest. She may conclude that her father cannot distinguish between restrictions on this type of information and her access to men; and she would be right 99% of the time.

But fathers know everything about boys that daughters want to know, and a lot more besides. They know all about the ways boys think about girls and how they behave. They also know why they behave as they do, although it must hurt dad to recall the way he used to think (if you can call it that) and behave. He is really the agent God intends to use to introduce his daughter to men, not the mother. It is a relationship that should continue all the way to the wedding altar, where he gives her away to another man.

Fathers won't be much good at this if they reject the fact that their daughters are given legitimate visions and interest in boys. Girls were designed by God that way because boys are related to marriage and marriage is God's primary means of fulfillment for a girl. It is her doorway of fulfillment and gratification in life as a woman, provided that woman marries the man God has chosen for her and provided she takes into the marriage the essentials needed to make it a happy one. Her father's participation is an essential ingredient to her success.

At an early age, say 10 or 11, the father should let his daughter know that he shares her vision. By that, he should describe it in enough detail to let her know that he is not, indeed, talking about a different vision than the one she has and he should confirm that the reason he knows it because it has been sent by God. She has not thought it up on her own. Hence, it has full legitimacy and is honored in her father's sight.

The vision she has is a romantic one, which features a knight in shining armor who slays dragons and storms castles for her sake, carries her off into the sunset, provides romantic fulfillment and sex, and receives the outpouring of herself upon him and their children. Certain features of the vision will grow as she grows.

The father also needs to let his daughter know that he has been commissioned by God to help her attain the full realization of her dream. How does that sound? Pretty good to most girls.

The father needs to set a positive tone that will help through some tough spots, where, try as he might, the father has a difficult time showing a positive attitude over some of his daughter's interests (and boy friends!). It will help if he can also provide more detail for her vision than she can do for herself, so that she can anticipate and recognize these details when they take place. Anticipation is half the fun!

For example, he should outline guidelines for dating through her marriage. Depending upon his view of scriptural protection and supervision required of unmarried persons and the quality and availability of Christ-centered youth programs, he and his wife might decide upon something along the following lines:

1. Dating activities will be limited to the social programs of supervised groups until age 16. There will be no "pairing off" for social dating prior to this.

2. Dating in pairs will occur according to parental guidelines with boys who "pass muster" with the parents and who show themselves able to abide by their guidelines. These guidelines

may include a considerable amount of group dating requirements. Additional plans may be required for post-school
employment or for college, later on, insuring that interested boys
present themselves to the father.

3. A special program will be put in place when the daughter
first identifies the man she thinks may be the one God has
chosen for her, according to the witness of her heart. (She needs
to be early prepared to identify this man to her father.) There are
three phases:

— the dating phase — special counselling, guidelines and
accountability with the boy; Father retains full sovereignty over
the daughter.

— the engagement phase (betrothal) — Father transfers
partial sovereignty over the daughter, with accountability of the
boy to the father extended to include this.

— the marriage phase — Father transfers full sovereignty
over the daughter to the husband. The father continues as a
counsellor to his son-in-law.

Dad also needs to set the precedent for the proper treatment of his
daughter. He should begin to "date" her at around age 10 or 11,
treating her the way he wants the boys who later date her to treat her.
This includes taking her out to eat, to the movies and theater, opening
doors, seating her, dressing properly and responding properly to the
subjects she wants to discuss. By the time she is actually "dated" by
another boy, she should know what the standards are to which she is
entitled and have enough discernment to recognize whether they are
being met.

Father also needs to schedule special talks with daughter and
mother regarding the essentials of her happiness; her relationship with
Christ, the ultimate Source of her security and happiness; the
relationship of the blood covenant of God in Christ and the blood
covenant of her virginity given to the man she marries; the importance
of her remaining unbonded to a man until her wedding night; she also
needs to understand the essential nature of the conflicts between
husband and wives, especially the effects of the fall of man upon their
behavior (in particular, the husband's tendency toward autocratic
dominance of the wife and the wife's tendency toward manipulative
compulsion and urging on of the husband, Gen. 3:16). She needs to be
led to an understanding of her own nature and God's prescriptions for
subduing it in Christ.

She needs to understand the horrific consequences of premarital sex, not only in terms of her own bonding with the man, but in terms of the loss of his manhood, which is her loss since it ruins the shield of protection which God desires to provide for her in marriage (and triggers the other threats to marriage discussed in Chapter Seven, "Loss of Manhood"). She needs to be given a vision of the powerful nature of her purity in inspiring and motivating her lover to protect her and ultimately enhancing his appreciation of God's blessing to him through her.

All of these things will also serve to establish her knowledge of her true worth. She will gain an appreciation of how valuable and regarded she is in the sight of her father. And these will be the standards she carries into her relationships with boys. She will seek someone who values her similarly.

When the "fruitpicker" finally arrives, the father, guided by his daughter's instincts, must be prepared to enter into a new relationship with the young man his daughter thinks God has marked as her husband-to-be. Daughter gets a chance to practice trust in her father before she has to learn it from scratch later on with her husband. The father's first conversation with the boy may be the hardest. There will be little equivocation, but plenty of gentleness, as Dad lays out some of the above precepts as they relate to his daughter's happiness. He must proceed to the place where he asks the boy, "Are you willing to cooperate with me and will you support this for the sake of her happiness, regardless of what ultimately happens to your relationship with her?" From there on, depending upon the boy's responses, the father will have to play it by ear. He should anticipate no trouble in discerning the boy's true motives and level of commitment to a dating program under his authority.

Guidelines need to be explicit regarding premarital sex, petting, or any situation which could lead to temptation in these areas which could defraud either the boy or the girl of the things God intends only for their marriage partner. They need to be discussed as explicitly as the father needs them to be assured there is no misunderstanding.

Rest assured, fathers and daughters, that disciplining of the boy for violations of any kind in his dating of the daughter are to be expected and must be enforced. The boy is unconsciously involved in following his own nature, which is primarily directed at establishing his own sovereignty. Do not worry about the effects of discipline upon him. It will only draw the boy closer to her. Daughter must see that this type of discipline is what God designed her husband to endure and that she must remain calm and trusting, allowing God to accomplish His will through those that are in authority over her husband without her interference. It is also scriptural for the father to discipline the boy for violations in which the daughter may have had a major role.

Hence, because of the bonding which will develop, it is also clear that the boy should not be permitted to date her at all unless he is a believer in the Lord Jesus Christ and shows evidence of having had a genuine conversion experience. The last thing a father or daughter wants is for an unbelieving boy to be bonded to a believing daughter (2 Cor. 6:14-16). If a daughter is unbelieving, her father needs to treat her as believing, knowing that God's promise is for her salvation through the father (1 John 5:14, 2 Pet. 3:9, 1 Tim. 2:3-4, Acts 16:31). If the father is unbelieving, then this whole text should appear as nonsense.

When a daughter becomes engaged, it is important for the father to extend and transfer some of the responsibility for his daughter to the husband-to-be, allowing him to have partial sovereignty over her under his guidelines. Guidelines regarding sexual activity do not change at all. However, other areas in which the daughter has previously been seeking guidance from her father may possibly be transferred to her fiance *to the extent the fiance is willing to submit to the authority of the girl's father.* The fiance should be seeking extensive direct counselling from the girl's father as how to address the questions of her continued education and/or potential employment, family planning, financial management and other areas in which he and the daughter will begin planning.

A right relationship between the boy and the girl's father developed during the dating period can develop toward a richly rewarding period in which the young man is encouraged and counselled in his responsibilities by a father who supports him and is the one other man in the world who has had responsibility for his girl's care and safekeeping, and who knows her thoroughly. The father can give the boy forewarning as to certain types of trouble he can anticipate from his daughter and how best to deal with it. The boy will also benefit from the father's years of experience in raising a family and keeping his own wife happy, something most young men learn purely by trial and error. He can get some of that knowledge from his own father, but the girl's father is in a unique position to transfer the knowledge he has gained in how best to deal with her particular personality, strengths and weaknesses as part of the process of turning over her protection and safe-keeping, as well. Praise God for His divine wisdom!

Hence, a period frequently marked by uncertainty and risk, the destruction of precious things not recoverable, secrecy, antagonism, and lack of support can, through the father's recognition of his "agency" on behalf of the daughter, become an exciting walk together for both father and daughter. Father can enter the vision and walk as a "deliverer" — the deliverer to his daughter of her nearly life-long vision of a solid, bonded marriage. Her father will also wind up as one of the continuing strongest supporters of her husband, working through an established support relationship. What a positive way to start out a marriage!

By this we see the continued operation of the husband and father acting as the shield in the protection of daughters until each attains to the "Chosen One," the knight in shining armor, the man whom God has provided them to fulfill their dreams. In Christ, they can continue the life God has given them together, submitted to each other and commencing God's plan all over again, reproducing their own good seed together.

13

The Two Fundamentals of Love: Mercy and Accountability

Blessed is he whose transgression is forgiven,
whose sin is covered! Blessed is the man to whom the Lord
does not impute iniquity...

Psalm 32:1-2

Everyone knows the scriptural adage, "God is love" (1 John 4:8,16). Unfortunately, because of our fallen nature and the modern distortion and overemphasis of romantic love, few know how to describe what love really is, and an attempt to elicit a definition of love's essential features will usually bring forth a confused response. Many are capable of identifying love only as an emotion. Certainly, love is not merely an emotion, though some would insist that emotions frequently accompany love. We see love operating without relation to emotions when a mother gets up in the middle of the night to clean a crying baby who has soiled his clothes, bed and floor. A father who continues to labor under foul working conditions in order to provide for an ungrateful, complaining family is motivated by something greater than his emotions. Both of these examples relate to the chief institution in which love operates in the human realm: the family. We intend here to discuss the family as a particular means by which to understand the fundamental attributes of love. God has given us the family as an institution not only to show us nearly unlimited examples of how love really works but also to start us on the road in developing an ability to perform its requirements.

The purpose of this discussion is to focus specifically on the two dynamics of love that underlie all of our actions, righteous or unrighteous, with those we love. These two areas are mercy and accountability.

Mercy says, "There is no further consequence of this action. You are restored and released." Accountability responds, "You will pay for your actions. There is a consequence for everything you do. You cannot go free without paying the account." In looking at the functions of mothers and fathers, we see illustrated in families how

God has apportioned these two areas differently by nature between men and women. He has done this in a particular way in order to fully illustrate the complimentary, though seemingly opposed, natures of these characteristics. By this means, children are enabled to experience and incorporate the reality of the dynamics of love into their own characters and to more easily comprehend how God perfectly combines and reconciles them in His own character in the execution of His plan of salvation in Jesus Christ.

Though corrupted and imperfect, we can see in reasonably normal mothers and fathers consistent and deeply ingrained behavioral patterns in the administration of the family that revolve around these two fundamental aspects of love: the ministry of mercy in the mother and the ministry of accountability in the father. The father is the one who says to his son who has just suffered an accident, "I told you not to climb up there or you would get hurt! Why didn't you listen to me?" The mother is the one who says, "Oh, leave him alone! Can't you see that he's hurt?"

Interestingly, few children will recognize their father's emphasis on accountability as having anything to do with love until later in life. Mercy is more acceptable and a child's preference is always for the form of love received from the mother rather than that received from the father. Yet each is essential if the child is to grow up with a reasonably balanced personality. If a child is exposed to either without the other, he will grow up with a badly twisted, though subconscious, view of God that will affect his own behavior. Mercy administered without accountability will result in a child's growing up without comprehension of the fact that bad decisions result in bad consequences; that wrong actions result in pain and sorrow. The child will have no bounds on his behavior and foolishly think that there will indeed be no adverse consequences to bad behavior as he grows older. He or she will become an unruly, rebellious child. ("Foolishness is bound up in the heart of a child; the rod of discipline will remove it far from him" — Proverbs 22:15. See also Proverbs 13:24, 19:18.) This problem most frequently occurs as a result of a mother having her way with the child at the expense of his experiencing the need for accountability as taught by the father, sometimes as a result of the death or divorce of the father. God says it will ultimately bring shame on the mother. ("The rod and reproof give wisdom, but a child who gets his own way brings shame to his mother" — Proverbs 29:15.)

Conversely, a child raised under an overemphasis of accountability without experiencing mercy will grow up with an embittered view of all authority and will similarly rebel. This most frequently occurs as a result of accountability by the father being administered at the expense of mercy by the mother, or as a result of the death or divorce of the mother. ("Fathers, do not provoke your children to anger..." Ephesians 6:4. See also Colossians 3:21.)

However, as out of focus and corrupted as each may be individually, these apparently contradictory characteristics come into close and supportive harmony when brought together in the family. The child sees and learns the reality of real mercy and real accountability. And in spite of human frailty, together the father and mother come as close to portraying God's character as anything we can find on earth. Indeed, most husbands and wives would agree that the other's behavior in these areas is as close to unfathomable as any other area of their lives.

A child who is raised under both the discipline of accountability and the mercy of forgiveness does not come to misunderstand that being forgiven or set free means there is no cost. As a boy who breaks a window should eventually learn, there is a price to be paid for that window, regardless of who it is who pays it. A daughter who breaks her mother's crystal vase should eventually comprehend that, even if she was freely and unconditionally forgiven, her mother paid dearly. In other words, a child raised under godly accountability and mercy comes to understand that true mercy means, "You may go free. I'll pay the account for your mistake." True accountability builds an understanding and appreciation of the price to be paid for our mistakes and a caution against lawlessness. It impresses upon us the fact that we ourselves frequently cannot afford to pay for our mistakes, and engenders real gratitude if someone is willing to pay for our mistakes for us.

Consider God, who has said of Himself that He is abounding in lovingkindness, who pardons all our iniquities and has removed all our transgressions from us as far as east is from west (Psalm 103), yet is righteous and cannot tolerate iniquities which have separated us from Him (Is. 59:1-2), even our own righteousness being as filthy rags to Him (Is. 64:6). How can He reconcile the apparent contradiction of His promised mercy and His promise of accountability for our sin? ("The wages of sin is death" — Romans 6:23.) What means are there in the promised new covenant (Jer. 31:31-34) by which He can satisfy His righteous justice while satisfying His righteous mercy to remember our sins no more?

There is only one means by which God can exercise such perfect mercy and still satisfy perfect accountability. That is for God Himself to pay the price for us, which we would otherwise have to pay to close the account on our iniquities. By sending His own Son in the flesh, He was able to render Him as a guilt offering (Is. 53:10) and provide satisfactory payment for our sins. In so doing, He simultaneously extended His perfect mercy. Mercy and accountability meet precisely at the cross of Calvary, upon which Jesus died. In perfect harmony with God's own character and purposes, He perfectly reconciled in a single righteous act the outpouring of God's righteous wrath on sin and God's righteous mercy on our need for forgiveness and healing.

We can see and understand this because we have witnessed it in our own parents and in our own behavior as parents with our children. Despite our imperfections, we comprehend that true mercy is always accompanied by someone else's paying the price for our mistakes, and that true forgiveness on our part requires that we pay the price for the mistake of another.

"If you then, being evil, know how to give good gifts to your children, how much more shall your Father who is in heaven give what is good to those who ask Him!" (Matt. 7:11)

14

A Husband's Intercession

Do not fear ... I am a shield to you.

Genesis 15:1

To a man whom God has not convicted in the manner of Judah, the following will be of no value. The suggestions are not formulae. Nor, if they were, would they be of the types of formulae into which any natural person, not in his right mind (the mind of Christ) would be able to insert himself as a digit. Nor would he have the faith to substitute himself for his wife, even if his love for her would draw him to do it, unless he also believed that God has placed him in the position of the shield. But prayers such as these are the exercise and the test in which restoration of a man is accomplished. These tests must be successfully met in order for a man to fully experience manhood.

The culmination of Judah's restoration was when he verbally appealed to Pharaoh to let him ransom his brother Benjamin with his own life (as an authorized and submitted substitutionary sacrifice) for the sake of his father (Gen. 44:32-34). He had offered it to his father before (Gen. 43:9), but in front of Pharaoh he faced the moment of truth as to whether or not he was really going to go through with his offer now that Pharaoh had declared his brother to be his slave.

He did it.

We as husbands and heads have the authority and position as shields to place ourselves as substitutionary sacrifices for our wives. It is our proper place as shields to do this; to take the blow *in their place.* We have authority according to the Word of God to offer ourselves to every kind of sickness, disease, or death in order to deliver our wives and children from the same. "Husbands, love your wives, just as Christ also loved the church and gave Himself up for her; that He might sanctify her, having cleansed her by the washing of water with the word, that He might present to Himself the church in all her glory, having no spot or wrinkle or any such thing; but that she should be holy and blameless. So husbands ought also to love their own wives as their own bodies. He who loves his own wife loves himself..." (Eph. 5:25-28)

Men, it is to no avail to argue that you cannot or do not need to take the place of Christ or to repeat His work for the sake of your wife, because He has already done these things on Calvary. It is your opportunity and calling to experience the "fellowship of His sufferings, being conformed to His death" (Phil. 3:10) by being obedient to the function for which you were created and designed. You are to identify with and be like Christ in all your ways, and with your wife that means being her substitute. You are to be a substitutionary sacrifice in her place.

For example, let's assume that your wife has cancer. You might consider a request as follows: "Heavenly Father, thank You that You gave me such a wonderful woman as my wife. I am amazed that You could have designed someone so perfectly to meet my needs for nourishment and healing. I am grateful for Your showing me Your love in the beautiful creature You gave me. Lord, I request that You would allow me as her shield to take onto myself the disease which now threatens her. You have authorized me in Jesus' name to be her substitute, to defend and protect her with my own body and life. I desire to do that and I do it now, knowing it may mean my death on her behalf. I know You are with me, Lord, and I am grateful for this opportunity to share in Your fellowship and the suffering You undertook on my behalf on Calvary. Thank you for this authority on her behalf in Jesus' name. Amen."

We do not know exactly the manner in which God will answer your prayer. But He will certainly answer. He may release you as Joseph released Judah, acting on his younger brother's behalf for the love of his father. You may be resurrected from the dead. In His mercy and provision, He has provided mercy for you in the broken body of Christ. Hence, His healing for your wife may be through your *having acted as the vessel* for passing the sickness onto the body of Christ, who is your Shield, according to divine design. Or, in the same manner that you could actually lose your life in physically defending your wife (as in war, or during a criminal assault), He may give you the joy of His fellowship and suffering in fully tasting your function as a man by allowing you to actually experience in your own body the disease of your wife in her place, to experience your mortal death. You would then know that your body has served its proper function according to its design (and that nothing has touched your immortality in Jesus Christ).

The mortal body is a "throw away," destined for corruption. Later, we shall put on immortality with the resurrection of the dead. Until then, let us assure that our mortal bodies are consumed and expended as God designed them to be.

PART II: PROTECTION

SECURITY
THROUGH ACCOUNTABILITY

...Be subject to one another in the fear of Christ.
Ephesians 5:21

...Put on the breastplate of righteousness...
Ephesians 6:14

15

Accountability

*But encourage one another day after day, as long
as it is still called "Today," lest any one of you be
hardened by the deceitfulness of sin.*

Hebrews 3:13

The Church has entered the age of accountability. While society gets more permissive and rebellion increases, its contrast with the true Church of Jesus Christ is growing. God is increasing discipline within the body of Christ. While this discredits the Church before the world, it serves also to discipline the Church and move it toward the purity we must have as the Bridegroom's beloved, "having no spot or wrinkle or any such thing; but ... holy and blameless" (Eph. 5:27). The body is also being disciplined regarding the generally shallow commitments and accountability to which we have been holding ourselves for each other's welfare. This is still lacking in the body of Christ (see Colossians 1:24). It is the body of Christ which is responsible for our brothers' fall. If we fail to discipline ourselves, God will use others to judge us. "But if we judged ourselves rightly, we should not be judged. But when we are judged, we are disciplined by the Lord in order that we may not be condemned along with the world" (1 Cor. 11:31-32). We must start with ourselves and learn to do this within the body.

It is ironic that the rod of discipline is now falling upon many who strongly wielded the sword of truth for decades. These have been men generally characterized as those among the early vanguard of the charismatic renewal. Many were seemingly obliged at the time to strike out on their own if they were to be obedient to the Holy Spirit. It "seemed right" at the time. In the 50s and 60s, denominational persecution of those who had received and ministered in the gifts of the Holy Spirit seemed to leave no other choice. Now, although these men may qualify as heroes who ran great personal risks for the glory of God and the benefit of the true Church, they have become casualties. Why? Was there an underlying cause? What exposed them to the evil one? Why did such strong discipline become necessary?

There is one common thread. It seems that they moved out from under effective authority. They went off on their own. They were apparently casualties to the common weakness of a lack of accountability.They consequently lacked an essential feature of protection that God intends for each of us.

The first recorded reaction of man's nature following the fall was to cover his nakedness with coverings of his own design and to "hide ... among the trees of the garden" (Gen. 3:7-8). God's solution was to bring what was hidden out into the open and apply the covering of His own design (Gen.3:9-21). We may be sure that God's solution has not changed and is still different from what man would design for himself (Is. 55:8-9).

God leads men to repent and to correct their failures by successfully walking pathways through which they had previously failed. Thus we see by example that salvation and righteousness are based upon men believing God, whereas Adam fell through unbelief. Boaz sowed righteous seed in the line of Judah and David by being obedient to the requirements of the kinsman-redeemer, which his ancestor Judah had failed to do generations before. We have the examples of Abraham, Joshua and Peter and their mistakes, used by God for our instruction. Scripture is filled with examples of men whose failures were used as stepping stones by God to aid either them or their descendents in ultimately "getting it right."

Hence, exposure to the nakedness of accountability is God's alternative to "hiding in the garden" to keep our sins from being exposed. The cure for the shame and secrecy of sin is transparency and confession; letting in light to avoid the dark places which harbor and protect the enemy. Accountability is God's wonderful protector against the deceitfulness of sin.

"Accountability" means having a life-style of "always being ready...to give an account" (1 Pet. 3:15), walking continuously in full expectation that one may have to do this at any moment and being ready to do it. It is more than lip-service. It is the mark of true servanthood, real leadership (Heb. 13:17), the doorway to greatness in the Kingdom of God (Matt. 23:11). Like everything else administered by God to the living, His chief agents for building accountability are men. Men must be accountable to men. A man who says he is accountable to God, but not to men, is deluded. He is greatly deceived.

Men are used by God as agents of accountability upon others, i.e., in judgment, but it is not because they are such great examples of accountability themselves. Men are typically great at holding others accountable, but weak in being held accountable themselves, demanding mercy for themselves instead. Their natural capacity to minister mercy to others is nil. Hence, it is important to understand that God's strategy and the true ministry of "accountability" is not served through holding others accountable. Although the capacity to do this in a godly way is an ultimate fruit, it is not a primary objective. It is last in priority. "Accountability" is primarily a spirit of *being* personally accountable. It entails the administration of accountability upon oneself, *understanding that it satisfies God's precepts for submission and provides protection against the enemy.* It leads in a direction which will ultimately increase one's capacity to hold others accountable without condemnation or in providing godly discipline, nearly impossible for the natural man or the immature Christian.

Then what is God's strategy? Like everything else in the gospel, it starts within the individual heart. One must receive the truth to oneself before being able to minister it to others. It follows the precepts of "destroying," "building and planting" of which Jeremiah spoke (Jer. 1:10). Men must first be changed in their area of greatest weakness and be replanted. They must become personally accountable.

In addition to personal protection, accountability produces fruit in the life of the person who walks in it through three additional precepts:

(1) Learning to apply mercy and bear others' accounts — mercy overcoming judgment (James 2:13),

(2) Development of discernment through the exercise of mercy and personal accountability (Heb. 5:14), and

(3) Reproduction of good seed through sowing (Gal. 6:7).

Hallelujah! Let us rejoice! We are on our way into one of God's richest gardens!

16

The Accountability of Spirits

For I, too, am a man under authority, with soldiers under me;
and I say to this one, "Go!" and he goes, and to another, "Come!"
and he comes, and to my slave, "Do this!" and he does it.
Matthew 8:9

In considering the whole area of accountability in God's economy, as it should apply to our own lives and always applies to the administration of His Kingdom, it is instructive to include the accountability of the spirits with whom we are in warfare, while abiding in Christ.

The spirits are subject to us, because they are subject to Jesus Christ, and we are in Him who have been redeemed from sin and death by His blood. Jesus said, "All authority has been given to Me in heaven and on earth" (Matt. 28:18). The enemies of Christ have been placed under His feet (Eph. 1:22; Ps. 110:1, 8:6), and His authority has been given to the saints (Mark 16:17-18, Matt. 10:1, Ps. 149:5-9) to perform the work of Christ in us. It is important to recognize that the spirits are always subject to our authority, inasmuch as they are subject to Jesus Christ and, indeed, shudder at the thought or occurrence of God's authority interfering with their activities (James 2:19).

The reason the disciples of Jesus Christ are not stronger in their exercise of God's authority in holding the spirits accountable and subject to the authority of Jesus Christ is that they have so little discernment of the presence of spirits and so little obedience in the exercise of accountability in their own lives. The two problem areas are related. God will not give us discernment and effective authority to exercise accountability over the spirits except to the extent to which we become accountable and trustworthy ourselves under authority (Matt. 7:3-5). Since all of us derive our need for God's salvation from a nature of rebellion, we are all in various stages of learning the godly blessings of being fully accountable for our actions. Indeed, we must all learn that God's protection and guidance in our lives, as well as His building of godly character in us, is based on the chief precept of being accountable under authority (Eph. 6:1-9, Col. 3:18-25, Rom. 13:1-7,

Luke 2:51-52). It is significant that God's chief instructions regarding effective spiritual warfare (Eph. 6:10-17) come immediately after comprehensive instructions as to how we are to work effectively under many different forms of accountability.

Once we align our attitudes and actions in harmony with God's precepts of personal accountability, He will begin to offer us opportunities to discern spirits free of the hindrance of those spirits that had had a rightful place in us due to our being nonaccountable under authority. (Rebellion is as the sin of witchcraft; it exposes us to spirits of the evil one to the same degree as does witchcraft [1 Sam. 15:23]). One of the chief of these hindrances is the spirit of condemning judgment which blinds us and makes us hypocrites in accordance with Matthew 7:3-5, unable to distinguish between the person in whom a spirit is operating, one who is the object of God's love and Christ's redeeming death, and the spirit himself. But as we properly practice righteousness and grow to maturity, our senses are trained to give us discernment of good and evil (Heb. 5:14).

The chief attribute of evil spirits that enables them to accomplish so much mischief is their nonaccountability due to their being un-recognized. They operate, in effect, incognito. Yet their power is almost entirely diminished merely with the recognition of who they are and by calling them by name. Once they have been recognized, they lose their ability to operate with a free license. They become accountable. Perhaps because the host's conscience is pricked by the truth, the power to further deceive is reduced (the enemy's primary power is deception). Or, once identified, it is possible to rebuke the spirit or pray a prayer of focused intercession by the observer in Christ. In any event, once the deceiving spirit has lost his shield of invisibility, he becomes almost powerless and is subject to the accountability and authority of Jesus Christ.

It behooves all of us who desire to become effective servants of our Lord, growing into maturity in His army, to come under the accountability that any good army must have to be effective. We must recognize that God requires all men to be subject to principles of accountability involving other men, depending upon the circumstances in which He has placed us, and that we must become fully harmonized and, indeed, purpose to support these principles in our daily walk with the people God has placed in our lives. Only then can we realize the righteousness and magnificent power that is released in the life of an accountable person.

17

Precepts of Accountability

*Therefore, take up the full armor of God, that
you may be able to resist in the evil day, and having
done everything, to stand firm.*

Ephesians 6:13

Convenient "one-verse" lines regarding the nature of accountability and our calling to it are few. Instead, we have a rich collection of principles and teachings relating attitudes of submission, principles of divine protection, the relationships of earth and heaven, and ministry of God's grace to those who will humble themselves, from which we may gather God's comprehensive instructions to believers. They are symbiotic.

The first important principle which relates to our need to be accountable to others is that *God never gives the truth through a solitary witness.* If we are to know the truth, we must have at least one independent witness verifying what it is we think God has said. This is based on the truth of Deuteronomy 19:15, which teaches that no matter is to be resolved on the basis of a single witness, but, "on the evidence of two or three witnesses a matter shall be confirmed." This is restated numerous times in the New Testament, included in the context of bringing an accusation against an elder (1 Tim. 5:19), exhorting or seeking agreement of a church member regarding sin (Matt. 18:16), confirming direction or a request in prayer (Matt. 18:19) and concerning anyone bearing witness of himself. It also applies to confirmation of prophetic messages from God (1 Cor. 14:29).

Jesus exemplified this when He stated the principle not only in general but even as it applied to Himself: "If I alone bear witness of Myself, My testimony is not true" (John 5:31). He went on to say that the Father gave other validating witnesses that what He spoke was the truth. One of these validating witnesses was a man, John the Baptist. The other, greater witness was the works which the Father gave Him to accomplish, confirming that the Father had sent Him (John 5:32-36).

The second principle is that *we are all responsible to encourage, reprove, exhort and instruct one another.* This is a reflection of a mutual responsibility of "horizontal" relationships within the body (as opposed to "vertical," hierarchical relationships which we are also admonished to honor. See section below). As many members of the body, we are responsible for each others' health (Rom. 12:4-16, 1 Cor. 12:14-27) and are told that we are to speak the necessary words of instruction and reproof to each other with all patience (2 Tim. 4:2), and to do this day after day, lest any of us be overcome by the deceitfulness of sin (Heb. 3:12-13). It is important to recognize that the words "reprove" and "rebuke," which we are encouraged to apply patiently to each other, are not negative words but are positive, just as is the word "admonish" (we are instructed to admonish each other in psalms, hymns and spiritual songs in Colossians 3:16). Hebrews 10:24 also tells us we are to "stimulate each other to love and good deeds." Hence, it is clear that we are expected to have visibility and access to speaking into each other's lives to enable us to support each other in love, speaking the truth for the purpose of building each other up in success with God (Eph. 4:15, 4:25). Scripture does not appear to exempt any members of the body from this.

The third basic precept is that *we are to carry with us a submissive and accountable spirit with respect to all of our relationships.* In Ephesians, Paul reviews almost exhaustively and in succession most of our major earthly relationships: wife-husband, husband-wife, children-parents, father-children, servants-masters and masters-servants (Eph. 5:22-6:9). He commences this review with the admonition to "be subject to one another in the fear of Christ" (Eph. 5:21), and follows it with instruction regarding spiritual warfare. Do you think it is mere coincidence that we are instructed in spiritual warfare immediately after such teaching regarding our being submitted to each other in our relationships? Not at all! The two are directly related. Things that happen in the spirit world are directly affected by relationships. Right relationships are more important than any so-called spiritual effort with God, just as Jesus told us in Matthew 5:22-24; reconciliation with any brother has precedence over worship of God. Husbands must also love their wives in an understanding way in order for their prayers to be answered (1 Pet. 3:7). God is saying that our spiritual lives will be held accountable to how we live in our relationships. "Whatever you shall bind on earth shall [have been] bound in heaven; and whatever you loose on earth shall [have been] loosed in heaven" (Matt. 18:18) .

Other admonitions to remain in an attitude of accountability are found in James 3:1: "...teachers ... incur a stricter judgment"; and Romans 13:1-5: "Be subject to the governing authorities ... for ... wrath and conscience' sake," and Galatians 6:1 "...if a man is caught in any trespass, you who are spiritual restore such a one in a spirit of gentleness; each one looking to yourself, *lest you too be tempted.*" The access of the enemy into our lives follows laws of accountability!

Jesus exemplified submission and accountability all His life, as did Mary, His mother. Even Jesus' growth as a teenager, "increasing in wisdom and stature," is recounted in direct conjunction with the only other Scripture we have on this period of His life. He "continued in subjection" to His parents (Luke 2:51-52).

It is especially uplifting to note that subsequent to her submission to the Word of God delivered through the angel Gabriel, Mary got all of her direction through her husband (Matt. 2:13-23). Her comprehension and freedom within the principles of submission are abundantly evidenced in the account of the wedding at Cana when she simply stated the problem to Jesus, telling the servants to "do whatever He says to you," and apparently walked off. Within this story, we see also that Jesus, despite the fact that He initially resisted the invitation of His mother to intervene ("My hour has not yet come,") *got His cue from the Father to begin His ministry through His mother, the chief authority in His life,* and was able to recognize this because of His submission to her. He responded with His first miracle (John 2:1-11). How many of us could recognize such guidance? Perhaps it was this sweet open spirit of accountability that caused Mary to be God's choice as the mother of Jesus and is so perfectly pictured in His responses to her.

The fourth principle related to accountability is that *destructive influences enter through those who are nonsubmissive* (i.e., the opposite side of accountability and protection is nonaccountability and destruction.) We see this in a vast number of Old Testament Scriptures, including Jonathan's falling under the curse of his father, Saul, through not telling him that he was attacking the Philistines. Although his failure to tell his father might have been inadvertent, the results nevertheless illustrate the consequence of nonaccountability. It led to extremely severe repercussions in falling under his father's curse and may have been a major factor in Jonathan's death (1 Sam. 14). Other examples include Cain's failure to heed God's instruction for sacrifice and to do right as a means of resisting the compelling urgings of sin. This led to his killing his brother Abel (Gen. 4:3-8) and his banishment. Samson's nonaccountability to his parents led first to the destruction of his family and later to his death (Judg. 14, 15, 16).

Miriam and Aaron's rebellion against Moses resulted in Miriam's leprosy (Num. 12). The rebellion of Korah, Dathan and Abiram (not having learned from Aaron, who received mercy when he repented) resulted in their complete destruction (Num. 16:1-15). King Uzziah was a good king until his heart became proud. Then his pride led him to refuse to be accountable to the priesthood for the proper burning of incense at the altar. He contracted leprosy and died a leper (2 Chron. 26).

Some of these sins might seem trivial and undeserving of such harsh consequences. But we see as an example for our instruction that even Aaron's mild questioning of Moses' authority ("Has God not spoken through us as well?") in truth reflected satan's characteristic of attempting to usurp the position of God, to be "like God" (Gen. 3:5). Hence the terrible destruction that takes place when we give satan such a place in us from which to operate his deceptions of usurping authority.

A fifth principle is that men, especially *those in authority, must be ready to humble themselves in order to experience the grace of God.* As exemplified by Uzziah, those raised to high position have a particular susceptibility to pride, which renders them useless to God. Only through their being humbled can they experience the grace of God. God's humbling is generally brought about either by disease or by bringing us to account by other men. Nebuchadnezzar was so humbled and ended up knowing and extolling the true God of Israel (Daniel 4). Naaman's cure from leprosy (2 Kin. 5:1-15) and King Hezekiah's facing of the Assyrian army (2 Kin. 18, 19) were tremendously humbling, but *also introduce the idea that a man's attitude can be shaped through exhortation and instruction to voluntarily submit to the process.*

Why should we be afraid of being humbled if it will bring forth the grace of God? "God is opposed to the proud, but gives grace to the humble" (1 Pet. 5:5). Behold how the wedding servants at Cana, taking orders from a stranger (and having been directed to do so by a woman, who was not even the hostess, at that), saw the miracle of the water's transformation to wine (John 2:1-7, 11). Nicodemus, a ruler of the Jews, humbled himself, coming to Jesus by night and getting some pretty strong words from Him for his pains ("Are you the teacher of Israel, and do not understand these things?"). But he became a believer and inherited salvation as a result (John 3:1-21, 19:38-39).

We see that God structures systems of mutual accountability to assure that we remain open and transparent to each other and able to be humbled if we refuse His provisions. Those who become proud require humbling if they are to be restored. Men who refuse to take part in the life of the body and refuse to submit to the demands of right relationship in a number of different directions experience the loss of spiritual protection and adverse consequences as a result. We see these principles established in the American form of government: the separation of the powers of the State, the elective process, the judicial process, etc., and we should see it in our churches, as well. But all of these higher forms of mutual accountability are without much benefit to us, except in restraining our lawlessness, unless we come under the self-government God intends through Jesus Christ. We must be personally accountable. We must flee to personal accountability, grasp it and put it on as a garment of righteousness.

Comprehend that our wives, our employers and supervisors, parents and governing authorities are all sent by God for our benefit. Love one another and work to each other's benefit. Let God speak to you and confirm direction to you through others, expecting Him to do it! Submit to the requirements of right relationships, being subject to one another in the fear of Christ. Be an active member in a body of many members, "not forsaking our own assembling together, as is the habit of some, but encouraging one another; and all the more, as you see the day drawing near" (Heb. 10:25).

18

Accountable Thoughts

*We are destroying speculations and every lofty thing
raised up against the knowledge of God, and we are taking
every thought captive to the obedience of Christ.*
Second Corinthians 10:5

Where are our darkest places, those unclean closets into which it is so difficult to bring the light of Jesus Christ? Are they not in our minds? Surely Paul was quoting the "bottom line" when he said we are bringing "every thought captive" to the obedience of Christ. This must be the most difficult place in which to bring the light of the gospel, the victorious strength of Christ and the healing power of His blood. How can it be done at all without the strength of mutual support in the body of Christ? "Therefore, confess your sins to one another, and pray for one another, so that you may be healed" (James 5:16a). Such things are impossible without accountability.

There is also an indication that the free and open ability to judge ourselves and to confess our needs, sins and weaknesses might even be considered the crux of accountability, since we are also told, "If we judged *[DIAKRINO; separate thoroughly, discriminate, discern]* ourselves rightly, we should not be judged *[KRINO; tried, sentenced, punished]*. But when we are judged *[tried, sentenced, punished]*, we are disciplined by the Lord in order that we may not be condemned along with the world" (1 Cor. 11:31-32). A reasonable objective for personal development in the body of Christ might be to be able to discriminate and discern ourselves rightly. But how will such discernment ever come to pass without accountability and discipline from others? It is clear that God intends such accountability by others to work for our good, to avoid condemnation with the world.

Every place through which water has coursed has carved its channel. Clean or foul, these channels invite their original hosts to again course their familiar paths. The mind is the place where the enemy established his playground before we came to Christ, and it is still his familiar haunt in which to pursue his corruption. We are in a reconstruction program in which these courses are to be reconstructed; they are being redirected to the light of Christ and made transparent. "...For you were formerly darkness, but now you are light in the Lord; walk as children of light..." (Eph. 5:8) We are to "be transformed by the renewing of [our] mind, that [we] may prove what the will of God is, that which is good and acceptable and perfect (Rom. 12:2).

It is important to grasp the extreme importance of confession in the process of the renewing of the mind and protection. It short-circuits *KRINO* (to try, sentence, punish) through self-discernment and opens the door to grace through humbling oneself. It is impossible for the enemy to maintain his deceptive power when his secret places and activities are exposed. God further promises that He will transform things that are brought to light. "But all things become visible when they are exposed by the light, for *everything that becomes visible is light*" (Eph. 5:13). In addition to the grace that is bestowed in the humbling of confession (1 Pet. 5:5), there is also the multiplication of power in a prayer of agreement of two or more (see Lev. 26:8, Deut. 32:30, Eccl. 4:12). How can one possibly obtain this power except through confession of his shameful secrets? Who can resist such promises for healing? Who could possibly prefer the darkness of their secret perverted thoughts to the healing of God?

According to God's Word, many can resist, because they prefer darkness. "For everyone who does evil hates the light, and does not come to the light, lest his deeds should be exposed. But he who practices the truth comes to the light, that his deeds may be manifested as having been wrought in God" (John 3:20-21).

Who can know the struggle of a man with corrupted thoughts to find freedom in Christ? How much must we pray? How many washings in the Word of God? Thoughts that didn't trigger the slightest pang before we came to Christ now oppress and frustrate our desire to be free. Initial lessons provide brief victories, only to end again in defeat! How many short-lived respites of freedom do we experience prior to grasping the folly of ever maintaining victory on our own strength?

In time we come to truly understand the truth of Paul's personal lesson regarding his own thorn in the flesh and what our Lord Jesus told him: "My grace is sufficient for you, for power is perfected in weakness" (2 Cor. 12:9). The weakness remains; it is how we gird the weakness with the strength of Christ that determines the victory.

How do we strengthen a weakened timber or a cord that is too weak, when destruction or replacement isn't an option? We lash or laminate other timbers around the weak one. Observe the multiple pilings of a ferry dock, lashed together with (multiple) cables, able to take the repeated blows of the ferries hitting them day after day! A cord is strengthened by adding other strands, doubling or tripling them until the needed strength is obtained. These additional timbers and cords are our brothers in Christ. We are to be individually members of each other, helping to hold each other up and bear the loads, "strengthening the hands that are weak and the knees that are feeble" (Heb. 12:12).

Jesus said, "My grace is sufficient..." Keep in mind that a man must be humbled in order to find grace. Many can grasp the concept of being joined to others for strength, but have to be literally dragged from hiding to apply it to their personal lives. We can humble ourselves voluntarily or God can bring about the circumstances to do it for us.

Lest we underestimate the difficulty of confession, let us consider it in more detail. A man has unclean thoughts. Before he came to Christ, he allowed his mind to become host to the spirits of pornography and his body to the vain imaginings of lust. Now a new creature in Christ, familiar spirits still leap from the pages of magazines and TV ads through their sensual images to invade his mind and torment him. Discipline against even picking up certain types of magazines provides a small measure of relief. But a man can't stop reading everything. News magazines, newspapers, billboards and TV strike at him before he has a chance to set a guard over the windows of his eyes. There they are again! Women in pictures and in the workplace! It's not possible to close *all* the windows. Where is our power to overcome the world, and not be overcome by it (1 John 5:4)?

Eventually the power of prayer is discovered and extended. Great advances are made in extending the freedom of the mind and the power of not merely praying for his own mind and freedom, but for the other person or persons through whom the spirits gained access. (See Chapter Twenty-four, "God's Provisions for Conquering Impure Thoughts.") For a while, as dependence and obedience to prayer is *increased,* he grows more confident. But now the power of the attacks also increases; temptations increase together with opportunity and imaginings that will not leave, drawing him, if possible, even deeper into lasciviousness! What happened to all the progress he thought he was making? Where is freedom? Has he not pursued obedience to Christ according to the applied Word of God? Is there ever any end to it? Over the weeks and months of struggle, another thought gradually creeps into his mind. "Tell your wife. Ask her to pray for you."

This is a show-stopper. Spirits fly to the defense of their stronghold!

"God forbid! My wife should be free of this! She would be crushed by the discovery! How can I possibly share with someone who thinks well of me these awful imaginings! How could she ever respect me again? I will get through this problem myself!" Weeks and months follow and the man's efforts grow more futile. "Who will set me free from the body of this death?" (Rom. 7:24) he groans. As his kicking and struggling diminish and his anguish increases, God again speaks. "You will never be free until you confess your thoughts and your difficulties to someone who loves you. Confess them to your wife and ask her to pray for you!" More kicking and struggling. Surely there must be a better solution. "Anybody but my wife! She won't understand. It will frighten her to know the enemy has had his way with me. It will take away her confidence in me!" More weeks go by. Again the groaning, "Oh God, won't You set me free!"

Again the words, now clearer than ever, "You will never have freedom in this matter until you present the matter to your wife and ask her to pray for you."

And so surrender finally comes. The dreaded deed is performed. Brought to exhaustion, the husband humbly tells his wife of his lascivious thoughts and his powerlessness over them. Despite the lessons he recounts having learned over the course of the struggle, he is still not free. If anything, he is worse than ever. Would she pray for God to release him from this bondage? She prays. Later she confesses, "Yes, it was difficult to see that my husband had these difficulties. I thought they only happened to other people. It did create some problems for me at the time."

But, oh, what victory they share! Incomprehensible freedom! Joy unspeakable and full of glory! Spirits of darkness are now routed in full flight, with no place to hide. No longer will they enjoy their advantage of isolating the believer. The light of Christ is illuminating their darkest hiding places. What a never-to-be-forgotten lesson in warfare! It will never be so difficult to apply again. Yes, such warfare does have to be applied as the occasion warrants, sometimes repeatedly. But now transparency and voluntary accountability are seen for what they truly are — a friend; God's means of bringing the truth to light for abundant protection, just as His Word says.

"Who has believed our message? And to whom has the arm of the Lord been revealed?" (Is. 53:1) Who understands that being protected means being accountable? Who will to flee to their wives (or mothers, or fathers or brothers) for protection? Who would expect to conduct any effective ministry without it?

Would you, dear reader, consider sharing your innermost secrets with those who love you and pray together in order to render the prince of darkness powerless?

Jesus, our ultimate example, transparent and fully accountable in addition to being able to bear the account of the Church, was able to humble Himself. He humbled Himself in coming to earth as a man and in going to the cross, and "did not regard equality with God a thing to be grasped, but emptied Himself, taking the form of a bond-servant, and being made in the likeness of men. And being found in appearance as a man, He humbled Himself by becoming obedient to the point of death, even death on a cross" (Phil. 2:6-8). He knows our difficulty in humbling ourselves and is ready to aid, "having been in all things tempted as we are" and "able to come to the aid of those who are tempted" (Heb. 4:15, 2:18).

He also had a support group of three men among His twelve disciples, with whom He lived transparently for three years, sharing with them all His innermost thoughts and activities. When under His greatest stress, He asked this group (James, Peter and John) to pray and keep watch with Him — just before His arrest. They were unable to stay awake, but the point is that even Jesus, except for His work on the cross, did not attempt to "go it alone." *He was transparent in His need and agony* and they became witness to His most anguished prayer for deliverance. We should follow His example and His directions and pray together that "we should not enter into temptation" (Matt. 26:37-45).

Just before going to the cross He washed the feet of His disciples and declared, "If I then, the Lord and the Teacher, washed your feet, you also ought to wash one another's feet. For I gave you an example that you also should do as I did to you. Truly, truly, I say to you, a slave is not greater than his master; neither is one who is sent greater than the one who sent him. If you know these things, you are blessed if you do them" (John 13:14-17).

Lord Jesus, please give us humility of spirit to be able to do these things. Help us be transparent with those You have given us for life support. Let us cling to each other in a manner which will bring Your light into our innermost recesses. Make us accountable for our thoughts. For as we know these things, we will be blessed if we do them. Thank You. Amen.

19

God's Provision for Accountability and Protection from Destructive Influences in the Church

1. Is one authority structure as acceptable as any other in God's view with regard to the administration of His Church?

2. If not, does God provide for a particular authority structure?

3. If God does provide for a particular authority structure for His Church, is there a judgment for failure to abide in it?

The above questions were posed to me by a man of God after I had shared with him what I characterized as a spirit of nonaccountability in my church with which I had been struggling for several years. Through these questions I was alerted to the fact that there might be scriptural causes for the particular set of problems I was facing, related to the organization of the church administration rather than merely the personalities of the individuals involved. This led me to a more thorough search of the Scriptures on the subject and conclusions regarding both the above three questions and the situation I had discovered in my church.

I submit these views as my own opinions and invite comment against the yardsticks of Scripture and personal experience.

There are several tendencies of unregenerated human nature that threaten successful leadership. It is useful to briefly review them to better understand God's provisions for protection against their unsubjugated operation even in those born again in Jesus Christ.

REBELLION: The desire of natural man to be independent, not subject to authority; to assume a position which is like that of God, in which he is subject only to his own counsel.

PRIDE: A view that natural man has of himself in which he places himself higher than or more important than others (with fear as to the consequences of being removed from this position, hence a protective rationale for its defense).

INSECURITY: The result of threatening circumstances to a person who views that security comes from being in personal control of circumstances, people and decisions which influence one's life, rather than from trust in God and obedience to His precepts.

God has made it abundantly clear in His Holy Word that He views rebellion against Him and failure to place Him in His proper position at the center of one's life as a violation of His most fundamental precept, and one which unleashes destructive influences (as those of witchcraft) into the life of the person in rebellion (See Ex. 20:3, Matt. 22:37, 1 Sam. 15:22-23, Is. 14:13-14). Our rebellious nature is supposed to come under the control of Christ after we are born again as new creatures through His blood, but pride and unbelief inhibit the rate at which we learn to submit our affairs and decisions to Christ. God also makes it abundantly clear (1 Pet. 5:5, James 4:6, Prov. 21:4, Prov. 15:23, Phil. 2:3-9) that pride places us in direct opposition to God and that His grace to us depends directly upon our willingness to be humbled submissively to the circumstances in which He places us. Finally, God also instructs us that our security is derived from trust in Him and obedience to His precepts rather than to our own hand (Josh. 1:5-9, Ps. 127:1-2, Deut. 30, John 17:12-20), and that clinging to the world's forms of security work directly contrary to receiving the blessings of God's Kingdom (Luke 18:21-25). In bringing us into conformity with Christ, God is constantly working to bring us to positions where we can exercise our will in harmony with these precepts, putting to death our old nature which still cries out in adherence to the old ways of the flesh. With this in mind, it is easier to understand what God intends in His provisions for the administration of the body of Christ.

The fundamental provision God has made for the protection of His people is that a local church is to be ruled by elders and administrative procedures which assure that "every fact may be confirmed by the testimony of two or three witnesses." The provision for elders and the underlying precept that no person is to be a sole authority for major church decision-making is seen in First Timothy 3:1-7, 5:17; Acts 20:28, 11:30; and Titus 1:5. The consistent provision God has always made for holding men accountable and assuring the best possible decisions through the testimony of two or three witnesses may be seen in Second Corinthians 13:1; Deuteronomy 17:6, 19:15; Matthew 18:16; and First Timothy 5:19. Adherence to this principle will assure the following:

1) Every man will be subject to authority (Rom. 13:1-3, Titus 3:1, 1 Pet. 2:13, 2 Cor. 13:1) .
2) Those who rule will be protected from pride and the condemnation incurred by the devil (1 Tim. 3:6).
3) Each person in the body of Christ will have recourse, when necessary , to hold those in authority over him accountable for their words and actions in accordance with Matthew 18:15-17 and First Timothy 5:19. In particular, he will have means of fulfilling Matthew 18:16 through constituted authority at levels appropriate to the grievance he may have.

Some churches have no elders. Others have their pastors under the higher authority of denominational bishops or other similar outside authority. Many have an arrangement wherein the pastor is in effect the only overseer or *de facto* church ruler and is not subject to any accountability other than that of his own conscience or that which could be brought about by factional efforts within his flock, involving other equally nonscriptural and destructive means of bringing attention to a problem. To the extent that any church departs from provisions in each of the preceding areas, it opens itself to destructive influences which will injure the body of Christ and harm the effective message of the gospel.

It is true that many pastors active as single authorities over their respective churches attain a certain degree of protection for their flocks and grace in the power of their ministry because of many hard lessons learned earlier in life wherein God has given them lasting areas of humility and attentiveness to obeying His precepts and personal leading. The requirements for efficient administration also frequently require single points of decision-making, including decisions at the pastoral level. The real issue in such cases is, "Is the person involved *willing* to submit his or her decisions to others on the basis that God has promised that He will make every fact known through the testimony of two or three witnesses?" Where there is willingness and trust to submit, there is probably also humility, faith and grace for God to work His pleasure in the servant. Where there is unwillingness, the opposite is true.

However, even though the pastor and others in the church administration are delegated authority to render autonomous decisions in certain areas of church programs, finances and teaching, assuming the above condition of willingness is met, it is important that a mechanism for implementing the possible confirmation of facts through two or three witnesses be set in place and *understood by each member of the flock*. In this manner not only will accountability be clearly established, but provision for the righteous behavior of other members of the flock will be made in the bringing of issues to light in the manner prescribed by Jesus Christ, without sin within His body.

God says that our leaders will give an account for themselves and we are to be obedient in submitting to, supporting and assisting them (Heb. 13:17). This is also consistent with the clear scriptural doctrine of mutual accountability between brethren. We are told to reprove, exhort and encourage one another daily, in season and out of season, while there is yet time, to work for the building up of the body of Christ (1 Thess. 5:11, 2 Tim. 4:2, Heb. 3:13, Eph. 4:15, 25). Where we are not held accountable to each other in the love of Christ, we will tend to stray like sheep, each of us to his own way. Where there is an unwillingness to be held accountable to those being served, there will also be a spirit of nonaccountability working to injure the body of Christ.

We help ourselves and build up the body of Christ when we learn how to hold each other accountable to our promises and commitments to God and each other in a spirit of love. If we fail to do this, God promises that the works of our hands will be destroyed. For He says: "When you make a vow to God, do not be late in paying it, for He takes no delight in fools. Pay what you vow! It is better that you should not vow than that you should vow and not pay. Do not let your speech cause you to sin and do not say in the presence of the messenger of God that it was a mistake. Why should God be angry on account of your voice and destroy the work of your hands?" (Eccl. 5:4-6)

Many churches today are suffering the destruction of the work of their hands because of their failure to adhere to scriptural principles of accountability in their church administration. Pastors and church leaders are bound to their habits and attitudes and have no means of benefiting from the blessings of accountability. Promises by members of the flock to serve, study, pray, and train in the functions of the body of Christ are made and not kept because of the opposing influences of satan. But God desires to use this for good in training us as overcomers through the application of His principles, one of the most vital of which is this one of mutual accountability, regardless of the position of the believer. Accountability will bring about several results: 1) knowledge and application of God's precepts to a greater degree than otherwise, 2) increased mutual confidence and trust among the brethren that their own building up is a purpose of each member of the body, 3) correction of errors, 4) steadfastness to obligations which cannot be abandoned without injury to the work of the individual and the body of Christ, and 5) protection from the deception and destruction of the enemy.

It is important, therefore, that each body inspect itself in its administrative procedures, attitudes and working practice to confirm that every person, including the head, is under authority and that procedures are in good working order for the confirmation of God's will through the testimony of two or three witnesses. The same procedures should be comfortably available to any of the brethren who, in obedience to the commands of Christ, have already gone to their brothers in private and failed to attain a response to their appeal for correction.

God's grace be on all churches and church leaders who prayerfully consider the application of these precepts.

20

Touching Sin

*...but from the tree of the knowledge of good
and evil you shall not eat, for in the day that you
eat from it you shall surely die.*

Genesis 2:17

Have you ever thought about why thunderstorms are fascinating, especially to children? What did you like to do when you were a child and you experienced a thunderstorm? Can you explain your behavior?

This chapter is devoted to assisting children. It may help them in their understanding of their motivations and dangers. It is useful for adults seeking to teach their children or who themselves need to understand certain things in their own lives before they can minister to their children.

There are questions such as these that parents can ask their children. Asked at the proper time and in a circumstance where the child has an opportunity to think about it and venture some answers before being given assistance, it should help in properly motivating them to seek the protection of accountability to their parents. However, to parents who have not learned accountability in their own lives, it will be very difficult to administer. "Do not be deceived, God is not mocked; for whatever a man sows, this he will also reap" (Gal. 6:7).

What about the thunderstorms? If you are like most people, you enjoyed going out onto the porch during a storm and listening to the roar of the rain and thunder without getting wet, seeing the flash of the lightening without giving it a chance to injure you. There was a slight chance that it might strike the house itself, but you couldn't help that. Going out onto the porch seemed to increase the element of risk just a little bit, but within tolerable levels.

What is the fascination in going to an aquarium and pressing your nose up to the glass tank behind which swims a huge, man-eating great white shark?

Why do people, especially children, enjoy being terrorized by a ghost story, or by going to a thriller movie, perhaps one in which even excessive amounts of violence, misfortune, death and destruction take place?

The reason is that we have a fascination with destruction and with the danger of destruction — as long as that destruction doesn't actually touch us! We like to get as close as possible to the experience, knowing that we are experiencing it only vicariously, not in our actual lives.

We wouldn't think of getting into the tank with the great white shark. Nor would we invite the terror and destruction of the horror movies into our own lives, to happen directly to us!

In part this is a result of the fall. We have a natural tendency to want to taste of the knowledge of good and evil and to think that we can do so without being injured by it. Some modern educators teach that it is good to teach your children about sexual perversion at an early age so that you can be in a better position to protect them. But this is simply not so. Our best protection against evil is to have no knowledge of it and to pursue knowledge only in the context of moral excellence (2 Pet. 1:4-7). We are commanded by God for our own benefit not to seek the knowledge of evil.

There is an interesting demonstration which you can do to illustrate this with your children. Take a piece of clean glass and, in the view of your children, hold it over a lighted candle at a level about even with the top of the flame. In a few seconds it will become covered with lampblack, or soot (essentially pure carbon).

Now ask your children (or students) if they would like to try to touch the soot on the glass so lightly that they don't get any on their finger. They will all be fascinated and want to try. Let them try it — over and over. They will never fail to pick up some of the soot on the ends of their fingers.

Now ask them to try to rub the soot off onto their other fingers and see what happens. They will observe that the soot doesn't wipe away. It *spreads.*

Sin is the same way. We cannot touch it without getting contaminated. And it spreads. God has a process for changing carbon into pure diamond. But it involves incredible temperatures and pressures. He can also work sin for good (Rom. 8:28) in the lives of those who love Him, but it involves incredible amounts of heat and pressure. After that the diamond must go to the jeweler to be cut with a hammer and chisel. This is hard on the poor diamond! God has plenty of this to do in our lives anyway, without our aggravating the situation by touching more soot! Let's teach our children to stay away from sin!

The awful truth your children face is that they are not in a movie or looking at the great white shark through a glass. They are in the world and in the tank. The question is, how do they avoid the destruction that is all around them and which they will see in abundance day after day in others' lives — immediately around them? Surely they know, in seeing their classmates at school, that many are destined for unwanted pregnancy, drug addiction, suicide, divorce and grief that defies all description. Are they going to be part of that? Or are they going to remain untouched?

How do they remain untouched?

A personal relationship with God through Jesus Christ is their ultimate answer. They need to be consistently taught the Word of God and led in this direction. But children have simpler forms of protection they can be taught to recognize and use at an early age. *Obedience to parents is God's most direct form of protection for children.* Parents are God's principle agents of guidance and protection, and children who learn to honor their parents inherit a promise of protection and blessing. "Children, obey your parents in the Lord, for this is right. Honor your father and mother (which is the first commandment with a promise), that it may be well with you and that you may live long on the earth" (Eph. 6:1-3). Note that this does not require that the parents be "in the Lord." It is clear from the ensuing verses (Eph. 6:5-7) that service and obedience depend upon the attitude of the server rather than the one being served, and that the one who obeys is to do it "as to the Lord, and not to men." (See also First Peter 2:18.)

Discipline of children does not usually seem to reach critical difficulty until they reach their teenage years, by which time effective discipline by the father becomes crucial. The mother is not designed to administer such discipline. By the time a child has reached these years, mother and father should be of harmonious accord in the manner in which mercy and accountability are administered. The father will be more and more challenged to seek God in prayer for answers to the unique problems which his children present for discipline. God will provide the answers to those who diligently seek Him.

A big danger children face is that they will run out from under their shield. Both the discipline itself and the relationship between children and their fathers needs to emphasize the special relationship between the father and the children and the fact that the children find their protective security from the father through accountability to him — they receive mercy, nourishment and healing from the mother, accountability and protection from the father. They must be substantively encouraged that accountability to their father is like a wonderful suit of clothes that makes them bullet-proof (even though on occasion not popular with their friends!)

However, just as God gives a father discernment in such things as knowing when his children are lying to him, so He gives discernment to children regarding hypocracy. Every father should recognize that the difficulties he confronts in dealing with the character traits of his children are rooted not merely in Adam and the fall, but are specific with respect to his own character defects, as well. God points out that we are always quickest to judge what we condemn in others because "we do the same thing ourselves" (Rom. 2:1-3, Matt. 7:1-5). When you face your children, you are looking at your own seed. The law of generations is staring you right in the face! What a wonderful built-in advantage! You can use your children as a roadmap to work on your own character defects while helping your children with theirs!

Get busy fixing yourself and God will do the work in your seed.

If you have refused to obey your own parents, dishonored that relationship or don't regard their counsel as being from God, then repent and get to work obeying them and listening to God through them. Work prayerfully and creatively in honoring them. Are your children intemperate in their eating habits? Take a good look at your own temperance in all things. Are they unresponsive and unfaithful in their studies, family chores, etc.? How are you doing in yours?

What we are saying is this. You, fathers, are the masters of the seed you produce. If you are concerned for your children's safety, then you also have the initiative and responsibility for instilling in them a correct attitude toward authority. Attitude is a product of the spirit; it is the spiritual seed which you sow. And you cannot sow seed which you do not have. Therefore if you want your children to be accountable and protected, learn to apply these principles to yourself. Then you will see well enough to pass it on to your children.

Such is the paradox of raising children. The understanding and motivation are in the parents, not the children. How are the children to respond to even the best teaching aids? It is likely that the best illustrations (such as "soot sin") and the most inspired lectures by parents will contribute only minutely to a child's understanding and motivation for the long term. But if you understand them, apply them to yourself. *You are the chief seed-bed for your children.* The lasting seed which works to their benefit is the Word of God. Plant it in your own life, water it and watch it reproduce itself in your children!

"Whatever a man sows, this he will also reap" (Gal. 6:7).

And stay away from soot.

21

Some Principles of Discipline

And, fathers, do not provoke your children to anger; but bring them up in the discipline and instruction of the Lord.

Ephesians 6:4

Ministering accountability means rendering judgment. There is no escaping this fact. Walking as a father or as anyone responsible for other people gives one the job of judging. We are accountable according to our office to render judgment and in this regard should not be squeamish over the accusations of others that we are being "judgmental." Nor should we misunderstand the Word of God on the subject. We must find ways to successfully conduct our stewardships of people as well as things, dealing with them as God has dealt with us and separating the sin from the sinner.

This involves learning how to discern the truth and how to discipline without denigration while bringing the offender onto higher ground. It is a difficult and thankless task. You may be hanged either as a sheep or as a lamb, but you will be hanged either way. Gratitude is seldom extended to a judge. The innocent expect acquittal and the guilty resent punishment. Only the repentant and regenerated can later experience the "peaceful fruit of righteousness" and perhaps belatedly look around to express gratitude to those who were their ministers of accountability.

There is much misconception regarding the use of the word "judgment" in the Bible, to such an extreme that one very popular modern reference Bible contains no other treatment of the subject in its chain reference than "Judgment Forbidden." No distinction is made regarding the numerous positive commands which we are given regarding judging, or the fact that the English language makes no distinction between "discerning judgment" (as in our need for "good judgment") and "condemning judgment" (as in "accusing," "convicting," or "sentencing"). The Bible teaches us to pursue one while avoiding the other. The subject is really much more complex than an admonition to avoid "judgment" altogether can support. "Is ... there not among you one wise man who will be able to decide [*diakrino*, separate thoroughly, discriminate, discern, judge] between his brethren?" (1 Cor. 6:5)

It is important to see that Scripture focuses primarily on telling us how to judge, as opposed to warning us against judging at all (Matt. 7:1). The reason we are warned not to judge is again because it remains true that we will reap what we sow. "For in the way you judge [*krino*, try, sentence, punish], you will be judged; and by your standard of measure, it will be measured to you" (Matt. 7:2). Hence, Matthew 7:1 is not necessarily an adage to avoid jobs and responsibilities which require rendering judgment. Rather, the combination of the two verses is an admonition to learn how to properly carry out any function of judging that comes with a responsibility, since we will ultimately be judged by the same measure in which we judge, and to avoid any judgment other than that which our office demands. Only people with no responsibilities can avoid the task of judging.

The man who becomes a father becomes the family's agent of accountability and is responsible for disciplining his children. This job falls naturally to the one upon whom the blows fall for the defense of the family. He bears the responsibility for the priesthood of the family and also renders the judgment over it in order to correct it and redirect it. Being the priest, he is tasked to discern and experience the consequences of sin in the family or his failure to judge it properly. This is his rightful position as shield as well as a guide to his approach to discipline. He bears the scepter of final authority over his family and will in turn be judged by Christ, who bears the scepter of righteous judgment over him.

We will presume this issue is already resolved in the hearts of those who have become fathers and focus upon the issue of how men are to carry out their office as judges without themselves incurring condemnation.

The major difficulty in rendering righteous judgment is that judges, judging as natural men, refuse to take any part of the consequences of sin onto themselves.

It is an inherent part of the thinking of the natural man that the person who commits sin must pay the full price for his sin. This is unscriptural. It does not reflect God's truth. Efforts to carry out judgment in this manner introduce destructive error in both the life of the one judged and the one judging and fail to properly communicate the gospel. Although such an approach does correctly convey the truth that there is a consequence for sin and that a price must be paid for it, it does not communicate the fact that sin causes consequences and grief in the life of others as well.

Also, although forgiveness and restoration are quite attainable and necessary as part of the disciplinary process, they will not have as great an effect in either life when the judge refuses to bear any part of the consequences as it will when he bears part of the consequential load of suffering and restoration. Only the latter approach can fully convey the love and commitment of the judge to the benefit and welfare of the one being disciplined and only this approach enables fallen men to learn to love with God's love.

We sense that this is a portion of the meaning given in Ephesians 6:4 in the admonition to fathers to bring up their children in the "discipline and instruction of the Lord." We know from the Scripture that the Lord Jesus Christ took our suffering onto Himself that we might be spared from death and the ravages of sin and be reconciled with the Father. This is the same type of discipline and instruction that we are to accomplish with our children. Children are to see Jesus in their earthly father, the priest of the family.

It is useful to spend a few moments contemplating why sin in the world is so rampant; why it so multiplies and amplifies itself in our lives and around us. It is because there are so few sin-bearers (outside of our families). Since the natural man always insists that the consequences of sin must return and fall solely upon the one whose "fault" it is, he is always engaged in active efforts to help the consequences of sin find their way to their "proper home." Ownership of sin becomes a huge rag ball which is added to and passed on. Each man adds his own accusations and proofs to ensure that the consequences of sin do not come to rest upon his doorstep, and so (in his own "righteousness") he contributes his own sin to the accumulated pile of dirty rags (Is. 64:6). He likely incorporates misunderstanding as well as self-righteousness into his arguments, never recognizing that he is not merely compounding the problem, but that the attitudes of anger, fear and resentment that have entered him are themselves also sin.

This all stops when someone enters the scene who is willing to take the sin onto himself. Eventually, if its effects are not to continue forever, the sin must be "swallowed." The consequences must be paid by somebody and the account closed.

Moses exemplified the person who takes a position of intercession on behalf of others in taking the consequences of their sins upon himself. When in the wilderness and informed of the sin of the people, Moses took the position that God should spare Israel rather than destroy them (Ex. 32:10). After pleading that God's reputation depended on sparing the people, Moses went further and took the position that if God could not spare the people of Israel, He should also take Moses' name out of the Book of Life. Moses probably did not know that such a position was unassailable; in his willingness to share the same consequences as the rest of the people, though he was innocent, he perhaps really thought that his request would be answered accordingly. He was no doubt unaware that he was representing the attitude of Christ, who would be our Sin-bearer, and that he would similarly (to Christ) be resurrected from this "death." We must have the same attitude in our willingness to share with those for whom we are responsible the consequences of their sin.

Any attitude that is short of God's standards falls short of the glory of God and is therefore sin (Rom. 3:23). Hence, we must recognize that a willingness to shoulder the consequences of another's sin is an inherent attitude necessary for rendering godly judgment. We are to judge as He instructed us "...not according to appearance, but with righteous judgment" (John 7:24). Following Jesus' example, this is accomplished by sin-bearing, i.e., getting "into the bathtub," so to speak, as Jesus did with us, to accomplish the job of washing off the grime of sin that has soiled someone else's life. In the midst of this we will also experience personal resurrection and see the glory of God.

22

Some Examples of Discipline

Foolishness is bound up in the heart of a child; the rod
of discipline will remove it far from him.

Proverbs 22:15

Theory is great, but what about application? Following are some examples that illustrate some principles by which the disciplinarian may share in the consequences of sin in such a manner as to bring children up in "the discipline and instruction of the Lord" (Eph. 5:4) as discussed in the previous chapter. These lessons did not come easily.

In one instance, individual children refused to cooperate and obey regarding their guidelines for watching television. The guidelines were that two-and-a-half hours per week of parental-approved programming were permitted. Within that guideline the children were allowed to select their programming and hours. Other television was prohibited. Months stretched into years of effort to establish obedience to these precepts, but these efforts became increasingly unsuccessful. The children developed increased levels of deception to circumvent the guidelines and many attempted remedies proved unsuccessful. Discipline accompanied with evident grief by the father, explanations of the consequences of sin, prayer with the children, reward and punishment, etc., and explanation of the reasons for restrictions upon television were repeated many times with no lasting effect. Cheating and deceit became rapidly-developing traits of the eldest child. After much prayer, and with great regret, the parents came to realize that only by their participation in the consequences of the sin of the children could the lesson be effectively taught. With appropriate final warnings, again disregarded by the child, the television set was put in a box and not taken out again for six months. No one in the family watched it during the entire period of punishment.

The oldest child, who was the first offender, learned her lesson and, to the parents' knowledge, never again willfully disobeyed the family precepts for use of television. Five or six years later the second child, a boy, approached the same age and exhibited the same behavior to the same extreme degree. The same form of discipline proved effective and those particular patterns of deceit never reappeared. The demon of television was broken in the home.

In a second instance, the son proved unable over a period of nearly two years to develop faithfulness in his feeding of the dog, one of his assigned chores. Because any failure on his part was quickly taken up by his mother's "filling in the gap" and feeding the dog instead (her nourishment instinct proved unalterable!) it proved nearly impossible to develop a disciplining scheme for him. Probably no array of alternatives has been as extensively pursued. It included posting of reminders, rewards, punishments (spankings, restrictions, etc.), and agreements between mother and father that should have produced some improvement, but nothing seemed effective for more than a few days at a time. Hours of prayer time were accumulated. Finally, the Lord spoke. "Let him experience the consequences of his failure as the dog experiences it. Deprive him of his meal when he forgets." The subsequent implementation of this discipline probably brought about more pain and anguish among the mother and father than any other before or since. It brought about a disruption of both the mother's and father's strongest family desire, the gathering at the family hearth — the dinner table. Even the contemplation of it was very difficult. But it was finally resolved and then explained to the son. "If you fail to feed the dog again, you will not be allowed to join us at the dinner table or have your evening meal. You will be sent to your room without supper." This final admonition was only good for a few days before the boy again forgot to feed the dog!

This discipline proved to be multi-faceted in demonstrating the truths of Scripture. First, the son reaped a fruit that was identical to that which he sowed. Second, he also suffered loss in one of the most powerful motivational areas of need of a boy or man — deprivation of food. But his suffering was slight compared to the consequences resulting in the third major area — the suffering which his parents experienced in the sharing of his discipline. The mother's heart desire to nourish her son was grieved; it was unfulfilled for the sake of his discipline. The father's desire to fellowship with the family around the family table was broken by the empty chair, and he experienced all the anguish of his wife as well. There is no doubt that the son sensed his parents' genuine grief resulting from this incident.

However, the lesson was driven home. The boy became a faithful performer of his chores of feeding the dog. Only once, more than a year later, did this lesson ever have to be repeated!

In another instance, it was discovered that intemperance in eating by one of his children was traceable to a root in the father. It did not reflect itself in overweight, but was there nonetheless. As years of futility in attempting to help the son gain control of his weight stretched out into additional years, it also became an object of intense prayer. The Lord revealed that no power would be provided to help the son with his problem of intemperate eating until it was repented of and disciplined in the life of the father. Hence, in this case, the father's participation in the discipline became the means of delivering his son from an aspect of the "law of the generations." A spirit of intemperance was held accountable. In this case, no words were ever spoken to the son regarding the father's repentance and the father became the sole participant in the discipline. The son was delivered from intemperance in overeating without another word being said or any other eating discipline ever being administered since that day!

There have been a few other occasions where the father's voluntary forsaking of his own meal at the same time his son is experiencing that discipline have proved very effective in illustrating that an underlying spiritual battle is involved. It is an extension of discipline which boys, especially, understand! The father's voluntary willingness to go without food for the sake of the disobedience of his son speaks eloquently of the grief of the father. At the same time it refines and disciplines the mind and spirit of the father in seeking God's answers to the problems being confronted.

Perhaps another reason this form of discipline is so effective is because it captures the essence of fasting in spiritual warfare. It is a form of "participatory management" in which the body, soul and spirit of the person responsible for discipline are brought into unity in "laying fast" to the issue. Resolution to enter the fray on such a scale until the issue is resolved enhances prayer, clears the mind and opens the communication with God for those seeking God's solutions. Double mindedness is removed and reservations which may have been previously present in the search for resolution seem to disappear when body, soul and spirit are brought into such unity of purpose.

As far as the child is concerned, such price-paying also communicates that the father is serious and committed to correction.

The examples we have discussed here illustrate that an effective disciplinarian must himself be under discipline. In rendering judgment and placing himself under his own judgment, a father must be focused upon rooting out sin from under his roof and from his own life as well as that of this children. These examples have dealt only with children of a family. What chance might we estimate for a man's ability to apply these principles outside his family for benefit to the body of Christ if he is unable to apply them within his family? Slim indeed, most would agree! Hence, we see the scriptural criteria of a man's need for demonstrated success within his family prior to his being placed in leadership within the Church (1 Tim. 3) and the acute need for us to learn scriptural precepts within the family before we can expect success on a broader scale in the Body of Christ.

The principles of discipline are the same outside the family, for those qualified to serve. Men who sit in judgment must be willing to place upon themselves the consequences of the judgments rendered.

Consider the story of an appeals officer tasked to hear the appeal of an employee who has been removed from her job and demoted two full pay grades for professional nonperformance and is now appealing the action. Over a period of years it seems her skills have deteriorated to the point where nearly every aspect of her daily work for a high level executive have become unsatisfactory. The disciplinary action folder, appeals material presented by her legal counsel and investigation folder are three inches thick, but investigation establishes without a doubt that she is, indeed, professionally incompetent at the pay grade at which she had been working and her dismissal and downgrading are justified.

However, another point arises out of the investigation. At no point in recent years has anyone responsible for her supervision ever undertaken to rehabilitate her. She has been maligned, embarrassed, condemned and mocked to a point where she has now developed strong defense mechanisms of denial, personality disturbances and paranoia in all her relatinships. She is isolated and defeated.

Yes, she is incompetent at her pay grade, but there is resounding testimony that management has failed to address her problem. How should the appeals officer judge?

While the appeals officer resolves that he must concur in the disciplinary action and deny the appeal, he also formulates the need for an employee rehabilitation program and structures this into his ruling. As he designs the essential features of this (schooling, counselling, a professional and personal support group for the employee, objective criteria with which to measure her performance development, etc.) two difficult thoughts begin to form in the back of his mind; first, the employee must come to know that she is loved as a worthwhile person and valuable employee, and second, only the judge who has perceived this root problem and its solution can effectively accomplish the rehabilitation of this woman according to this plan. Increasingly, his thoughts became, "Why don't you do it yourself?" "Make her your secretary!" (His response: "Not me, Lord! Besides, You know my secretarial position is already filled!")

Two days later, after completing his plan, the appeals officer's secretary suddenly submitted two week notice that she had accepted a better job. His secretarial position was now open!

The lessons given in God's classroom are not easy. Certainly the appeals officer's attitudes were considerably tested by God's action to give him the direct responsibility for this woman's rehabilitation. He was required to get into the tub himself to get the job done! Great difficulties followed. But out of them came a new relationship with the employee and her husband, her successful rehabilitation (proved and ultimately validated under separate executive supervisors), restoration to her original pay grade and her salvation in Jesus Christ. It was a work of God, enabled by the judge sharing in the purification and healing process!

Consider now an example of what may be ultimately involved in giving children wisdom. "The fear of the Lord is the beginning of wisdom" (Ps. 111:10). The Bible also says that "the fear of the Lord is the beginning of knowledge" (Prov. 1:7). What father does not desire to give his children knowledge and wisdom before their leaving home? Ultimately, responsibility for discipline must be released from parent to the Lord and children must leave home with the fear of the Lord. This may come down to specific prayers for God to intervene and establish His personal relationship with the children in a fashion that ensures the reverence and respect for God they need, if they have not previously come to it. This proved to be the case in the author's life when it became painfully evident that his 17-year-old son had no such fear of God. Prayers went out for God to intervene personally.

One evening our son went off to spend the night at his sister's house. For some reason, we had occasion to call her later that evening, discovering that our son had not arrived, nor had she known of any plans on his part to stay overnight! The jig was up! But where was our son? It turned out that he had gone to an all-night party and had only planned to put in a token appearance at his sister's house before coming home the next morning. However, when he came out from the party at 5:00 AM, he found that the police had towed the family car! In an effort to hold his story together, he then solicited a ride from a friend to his sister's place halfway across the city, only to discover from his sister upon arrival that his cover was already blown! Things further unravelled into what proved to be a very expensive price that our son ultimately paid for this adventure. Yet his punishment was relatively inconsequential compared to his discovery that God had so cooperated with his parents to expose his deception. What a priceless discovery! "For whom the Lord loves, He disciplines!" How much better to be disciplined as a son than left alone as an illegitimate child! (Heb. 12:6-8)

The bottom line issue is our heart. God's Word is able to discern the thoughts and intentions of the heart (Heb. 4:12). "All the ways of a man are clean in his own eyes. But God judges the motives" (Prov. 16:2). We will be judged by our motives, not our actions. Hence we must love the ones we are disciplining, desiring their very best, their advancement, their success with God. This becomes our motivation and points us to the laying down of our lives.

Remember how we will be judged. If we are angry and condemning when we execute discipline, then that is how God will judge us (Matt. 7:2). It is ironic that our children are learning from us while we are ourselves learning to teach them; that we are all children learning together according to God's design. Mistakes are not inappropriate. God has designed it this way to give us all multiple opportunities, with motivation to "get it right" and to learn as easily as possible with the people we love and to benefit from our many mistakes. Let's keep working and praying together and supporting each other in His Word to do this for Jesus' sake. Amen.

"Never pay back evil for evil to anyone. Respect what is right in the sight of all men" (Rom.12:17).

"And just as you want men to treat you, treat them in the same way" (Luke 6:31).

23

Reconciliation with Fathers

Now all these things are from God, who reconciled us to Himself through Christ, and gave us the ministry of reconciliation, namely, that God was in Christ reconciling the world to Himself, not counting their trespasses against them, and He has committed to us the word of reconciliation. ...We beg you on behalf of Christ, be reconciled to God.

Second Corinthians 5:18-20

Many believers are unfamiliar with these words, although they are very familiar with the Scriptures directly on either side of these. These are: "Therefore if any man is in Christ, he is a new creature; the old things passed away; behold, new things have come" (2 Cor. 5:17); "He made Him who knew no sin to be sin on our behalf, that we might become the righteousness of God in Him" (2 Cor. 5:21).

Why is it that two of the most well-known Scriptures in the Bible contain in their midst three other verses on reconciliation which are almost never quoted with them and are hardly known?

Perhaps it is because they come with a strong attendant admonition that salvation means reconciliation and most men find it too difficult to accept the demands of reconciliation in their personal lives.

The basic problem of the universe is "father-rejection"; the break in relationship between men and the Father. The most common manifestation of it is the break in relationship between children and their earthly fathers. This is what Jesus came to solve. Even among believers, reconciliation between children and their earthly fathers remains difficult and has been for too long unaddressed. What should bring shouts of rejoicing — "Hallelujah!" — brings from most men only a groan and tight-lipped certitude that "no one could be reconciled with *my* father." But, praise God, this is not true. Fathers are the centerpiece of reconciliation!

God wants us each to be reconciled and fathers are at the head of His list. When reconciliation breaks out, God highlights the fact that it will feature fathers. This will mark the end of the age! The last verse in the Old Testament reads, "And he will restore the hearts of the fathers to their children, and the hearts of the children to their fathers, lest I come and smite the land with a curse" (Mal. 4:6). Our earthly fathers are the closest earthly facsimile to our heavenly Father for the major illustrations of the New Testament (Matt. 6:9, Luke 15:11-32, Heb. 12:7-10). Our progress at fellowship with God will remain stunted until we receive His reconciliation with our earthly fathers.

The responsibility is ours, not our fathers'. Children are commanded to honor their parents, not vice versa. Furthermore, our well-being is tied to obedience to this command. As Paul said, "Honor your father and your mother (which is the first commandment with a promise), that it may be well with you, and that you may live long on the earth" (Eph. 6:2-3).

Evidence of broken relationships with fathers shows up immediately in counseling men who have a string of other broken relationships with employers and those in authority. A son's inability to maintain accountability with his father is carried into all other relationships which demand accountability. Furthermore, that inability to put into practice any concept of working to please an earthly father results in employment attitudes that are totally self-centered; the idea of working to enhance his employer's goals and financial success are totally foreign and almost incomprehensible to such a man. Hence, a correct attitude of servanthood should be rooted in service to his father. If he has an incorrect attitude, it must be corrected.

We should note that, although the brother of the prodigal son did not comprehend the grace and forgiveness of his father, he could not be faulted for his own wonderful attitude in faithfully serving him! It might be a safe bet that he was able to hear the admonition of his father and adjust his attitude when his father reproved him (Luke 15:31-32) because of their basically sound relationship. Jesus also pointed this out in the parable of the two sons, one of whom said he would obey but did not, and the other who said he would not obey but later did (Matt. 21:28-31). It was the *actions* that ultimately counted, not the initial response or words. We still have the chance to get it right!

Fathers have good reason to get to work on this problem if they remain in poor relationship with their own fathers. For "God is not mocked; whatever a man sows, this he will also reap" (Gal. 6:7). This does not mean that the father with the bad relationship with his father needs to focus his attention on his relationship with his children in order to avoid having the same problem with them. No, it means he must develop a good relationship *with his father!*

The roots of rejection of fathers are in bitterness (unforgiveness for grievances caused by the father), immorality or godless values (i.e., a worldly value system [Heb. 12:15-16]), which may also stem from father. These lead to rebellion which open children up to destructive spirits of the enemy equivalent to those of witchcraft that gain legal access to anyone not remaining under the protective cover of accountability (1 Sam. 15:23).*

But the same Scriptures that warn us against these sins also advise us that no one is to fall short of the grace of God. How do we assure this? The grace of God is in humbling ourselves by forgiving and by seeking forgiveness! By reconciliation! It is a first order of business in God's sight. "If therefore you are presenting your offering at the altar, and there remember that your brother has something against you, leave your offering there before the altar, and go your way; first be reconciled to your brother, and then come and present your offering" (Matt. 5:23-24). If this is the instruction of Jesus for brothers, what do you suppose it is for fathers?

Men are notoriously poor in the area of asking for forgiveness. It is especially hard to humble oneself before your own father because you have inherited so many traits from him. You know him thoroughly and dislike every one of his unpleasant traits that has been passed on to you (Rom. 2:1-3). But asking forgiveness is difficult in most instances, anyway, and so some instruction is useful. The following points should be applied:

a) Prepare. Pray for God to free you from deception and to show you your specific sins in a fashion that will enable you to confess and take responsibility for them. This is not to be "eyewash"! Ask the Lord for humility and grace.

b) Rehearse your apology, word for word, with another witness. Another witness can scrutinize your spirit for compromise and the presence of deceiving spirits which would keep us from a full confession of our sin and responsibility. For the same reasons, it is best to write it down oneself even before this rehearsal. Working with a witness also helps to maintain steadfastness of purpose (by increasing our accountability to another person) and follow-through. The prodigal son rehearsed his statement of repentance to his father *word for word, beforehand.*

c) Make no reference whatsoever to anything the other person (father) has done to you, either directly or by inference.

---

* *Excellent instruction, testimony and scriptural insight on this subject is offered by Bill Gothard and the Institute in Basic Life Conflicts (Box 1; Oak Brook, IL 60521).*

Forgive that beforehand. If you find it difficult, write the offenses down on a separate piece of paper, forgive them and close the account by asking God to also forgive them and close the account in heaven (Matt. 18:18, John 20:23). Then burn the statement of offense and never bring it up again. "Love does not keep an account of wrongs suffered" (1 Cor. 13:5).

d) Be specific in stating the offenses which God has impressed upon you and be specific in asking for forgiveness.

As an illustration of how confusing and difficult it may be to pursue responsibility for confession of sin and asking forgiveness (especially from one's father), following are quotes from two letters which a man named Richard (in his mid-30s) wrote to his father. The first one came as a draft for review a few days after a good counseling session had brought about conviction and a desire to approach the father with a request for forgiveness. It read, "Dad, if I have done anything in my past that has hurt you, I am sorry. Please forgive me." It was clear that between the counseling session and the time of writing the letter, interfering spirits and a certain crisis of purpose had entered the picture!

Weeks letter, however, after further counseling pointed out the shortcomings of the first approach (and the counselor thought his efforts had failed) Richard wrote this:

Dear Dad,

I am writing this letter so that all that is important will be said. I am not sure I would get everything in the proper order and all that is on my heart said if I talked with you face to face first.

Dad, God has convinced me that I've been a poor son to you and failed to honor you as I should. I know for a fact that when I was young, I always thought that you were wrong when you were giving me advice or direction, so I always disobeyed you or counted your advice as worthless. I know now that you were right most of the time, but I never benefited from it because of my rebellion.

God calls my rebellion sin. I'm convinced that God is right and I have suffered because I never listened to you.

I know also that you have tried your best to be a good father to me and I've never shown any appreciation for that. I'm grateful that God gave me you as my father and I want to be a better son. I'm also grateful that you never punished me as I really deserved. Will you forgive me?

If you have anything you want to share with me, I am ready and willing to listen and take your advice from here on out.

I love you with all my heart.

Richard

Hear the Holy Spirit! Praise God for His grace and forgiveness. This first step produced a powerful change in that relationship and further growth in Christ in Richard that has enriched his life and strengthened other important relationships in his life, as well. If other men can't do better after an appropriate period of effort, they wouldn't do badly to use this letter as a model!

24

God's Provisions for
Conquering Impure Thoughts

For the creation was subjected to futility, not of its own will, but because of Him who subjected it, in hope that the creation itself also will be set free from its slavery to corruption into the freedom of the glory of the children of God.

Romans 8:20-21

Probably no other problem afflicts so many men as the problem of unclean thoughts in the minds of those who have come to Christ. In the cesspool of their vain imaginings, the enemy torments and oppresses the adopted sons of God with frustration over the seeming evidence that God does not have the power to cleanse their thought life and provide them with true freedom. The more mature they become in their walk of discipleship, the more acute and frustrating this problem becomes. Men of Christ want to be free, but seem to be unable to gain victory for more than a few hours or days at a time. The problem is more widespread now than ever before because of the spreading filth of our society and the dramatic spread of sexual corruption throughout the families of America. It is an awful stench that has fouled our lives for too long, now erupting in our society in the most heinous of crimes against women and children.

There are many foul pictures with which the enemy torments us, not limited to the example around which the prescriptions of this chapter are focused. They can be equally applied to the problems of fear or hatred of a neighbor, unforgiveness, envy, coveting and many others of the evil thoughts which proceed out of the mind of man which defile him (Mark 7:21-23). But in learning to "bring every thought captive to obedience to Christ," it is useful to apply the principles of victorious warfare to the area which is probably the most common problem among men and in which continued defilement has been most directly destructive to manhood. We desire to hold these spirits accountable and rid them from our midst — therefore let us *BE* accountable!

We have seen too many pictures, too many films, too much TV and been involved in too much immorality and filthiness to simply close down the pictures of our minds. There are huge caves of residence established in our minds in which the enemy was once entertained; he secured legitimate access. Now it seems impossible to close the doors to him. Demonic spirits leap across magazine pages, city streets, restaurants and everyday work places to pursue the stimulation of old evil thought habits. They seem to be everywhere. How does one resist them? Is there any hope of gaining permanent victory over them?

Yes there is, in Christ Jesus.

But we must first learn to stay with our Lord and Shepherd. Having hearts of sheep, we tend constantly to go astray, wandering off on our own. Each victory tends to take us away from the Source of our victory.

It is the incorrect and powerful thought habit of the "old man" that tells us we experience freedom when we are independent. This is not true at all. We find our freedom by becoming bond-slaves to Jesus Christ. It is when our thoughts become *captive* to Christ that we bring down the strongholds and [destroy] speculations and every lofty thing raised up against the knowledge of God..." (2 Cor. 10:5)

But when we find a temporary solution to being unoppressed, we tend naturally to revert to going our own way, only to fall into the same trap all over again. Both the independent behavior and the weakness are symptomatic of the natural man. It is this weakness that delivers us to Christ again and again, teaching us to stay with Him.

Remember Paul's lesson in his attempts to get free of the thorn of his flesh. He was finally given specific instructions by the Lord. "My grace is sufficient for you, for power is perfected in weakness." Paul's response was that he would most gladly boast in his weaknesses, that the power of Christ could dwell in him (2 Cor. 12:9).

This is spiritual warfare. It is actual and demanding combat. Praise God that Jesus has secured the victory in our weakness! You will share in this victory as you practice (as any warrior) until you become so skilled in the wielding of your weapons that the enemy sees only the prospects of defeat and a net loss every time he attempts to breach your defenses. As the swing of your sword, the Word of God (Eph. 6:17), becomes more consistent, you will experience freedom. You will come to rejoice at each opportunity to see time-proven principles of warfare do more than provide you with victory. You will see the hand of God gaining new territory for Christ.

One of the things a warrior should always seek in combat is to go on the offensive. We are seeking to gain new territory for the Kingdom of the Lord Jesus Christ and should not be content to play defense or stay in the middle of the field. Nothing is as painful for the enemy or joyful for the child of God as discovering that the enemy's efforts to assail your defenses has resulted in net losses to his territory of darkness. We do not wish merely to win. We want the enemy to lose! *Hence, in the prescriptions which follow, pay special heed to those areas in which you go on the offensive.*

View every occasion of combat as the opportunity to go on the offensive and bring the light of God into someone else's life "...to build and to plant" (Jer. 1:10).

The following scripturally-supported scenario of spiritual combat will bring victories which must be experienced to be appreciated. They need personal discovery. God's power is available to support His warriors:

1. Commence every occasion in which you are assailed with unclean thoughts with praise to God, for you know He has purposed and provided that you are to have a clean mind. Memorize and speak to God your personal knowledge of this based on the following Scriptures (which have been changed to first person for personal application):

● "Sin shall not be master over me, for I am not under law, but under grace" (Rom. 6:14).

● "I shall know the truth, and the truth shall make me free" (John 8:32).

● "I am not being conformed to this world, but am being transformed by the renewing of my mind, that I may prove what the will of God is, that which is good and acceptable and perfect" (Rom. 12:2).

● "In reference to my former manner of life, I am laying aside the old self, which is being corrupted in accordance with the lusts of deceit, and am being renewed in the spirit of my mind" (Eph. 4:22-23).

● "I am to be perfect, as my heavenly Father is perfect" (Matt. 5:48).

Thank God again that these things are true and that they will prevail in your life because His truth shall stand after everything else has passed away.

2. Review and acknowledge the work of the Holy Spirit in your life to guard the windows of your soul. The Holy Spirit will be working and is working at this very moment in having convicted you and

brought you to this point of prayer and spiritual warfare. He desires to fulfill the use of your eyes as righteous lamps of light, fulfilling the law of Christ in you and removing the curse of failure from you.

• "I have made a covenant with my eyes; how then could I gaze at a virgin?" (Job 31:1)

• "The lamp of my body is my eye; when my eye is clear, my whole body also is full of light; but when it is bad, my body also is full of darkness" (Luke 11:34) .

• "Sheol and Abaddon are never satisfied, nor are the eyes of [a natural] man ever satisfied" (Prov. 27:20).

3. Recognize that your warfare is truly with spirits and *not with the person or persons through which the tormenting spirits have gained your eyes or mind.* You are going to use this understanding to pray on behalf of the person or persons in a few moments. You are going to prevail over the spirits which assail the "lust of the flesh, the lust of the eye and the pride of life" (1 John 2:16) by praying on behalf of this person or persons. Memorize and review the applicable Scriptures:

• " I stand strong in the Lord, and in the strength of His might. I put on the full armor of God, and am standing firm against the schemes of the devil. For my struggle is not against flesh and blood, but against the rulers, against the powers, against the world forces of this darkness, against the spiritual forces of wickedness in the heavenly places" (Eph. 6:10-12; learn verses 13-18 as well).

• "The weapons of my warfare are not of the flesh, but divinely powerful for the destruction of fortresses. I am destroying speculations and every lofty thing raised up against the knowledge of God, and I am taking every thought captive to the obedience of Christ" (2 Cor. 10:4-5).

4. If you entertained and gave audience to the spirits which brought these unclean pictures to your mind, then apply the blood of Jesus onto them by actually speaking the words of application of the blood of Jesus. Receive forgiveness and healing and express your faith in the effectiveness of this by thanking God for both forgiveness and healing. Memorize and apply the following Scriptures:

• "[Jesus] Himself bore my sins in His body on the cross, that I might die to sin and live to righteousness; for by His wounds I am healed" (1 Pet. 2:24) .

• "In Him, I have redemption through His blood, the forgiveness of my trespasses, according to the riches of His grace" (Eph. 1:7).

- "For if the blood of goats and bulls and the ashes of a heifer sprinkling those who have been defiled, sanctify for the cleansing of the flesh, how much more will the blood of Christ, who through the eternal Spirit offered Himself without blemish to God, cleanse my conscience from dead works to serve the living God?" (Heb. 9:13-14)

- "I am a brother of the Lord Jesus Christ (Rom. 8:29, Heb. 2:17); and I overcome the accuser [satan] because of the blood of the Lamb and because of the word of my testimony and because I do not love my life even to death" (Rev. 12:11).

5. Review the fact that you are a warrior who expects to go into battle. This is normal since you are in a war. You are going to win and you expect to win. Recognize that you are growing stronger and more skilled every day you engage in this combat. Not only this, but as you regularly exercise, you are developing powers and gifts of discernment that God has given you. Memorize and personally apply the following scriptural facts:

- "I am like Daniel. I have resolved not to defile myself" (Dan. 1:8).

- "I am putting on the Lord Jesus Christ, and make no provision for the flesh in regard to its lusts" (Rom. 13:14).

- "I am becoming a mature warrior, able to eat solid food and who, because of my practice, have my senses being trained to discern good and evil" (Heb. 5:14).

- "I am running now against footmen and will not tire out so that, as I grow in the Lord, I can successfully compete with horses" (Jer. 12:5).

- "I have a host of witnesses. I am laying aside this sin and every one which would encumber me to run the race that is set before me. I welcome the discipline this is developing in me in training me in righteousness and I recognize it as a sure mark of my Father's love for me" (Heb. 12:1-12).

6. Use the occasion of sensual or unclean thoughts as your signal for offensive operations against the enemy on behalf of the person through whom the attack was made (in picture, person, or dream). Cover the following points in asking specifically for:

—a hedge of thorns to protect that person from destructive influences (Hos. 1);

—blessings for that person in good relationships, health, finances, security, etc.;

—salvation; a saving knowledge of the Lord Jesus Christ;

—a rich relationship and blessed life in the Lord Jesus Christ; and

—a righteous relationship between that person and yourself that would meet God's scrutiny and the scrutiny of man — your wife and your parents.

NOTE: This particular portion of your actions in response to coming under spiritual attack is the most important regarding your growth in Christ and in gaining freedom from the enemy. As you pursue this prayer request, you will experience miraculous transforming power in your thoughts and attitudes toward the person involved. Assuming you have been attacked with sensual thoughts through a woman, you might pray along the following lines:

Dear Heavenly Father,

Thank You for the life of this girl. Thank You for the knowledge that You created her and love her; that Jesus died for her and seeks to have a wonderful and righteous relationship with her that will bring her eternal life and blessings beyond number. Father, I ask on her behalf that you would protect her from the destructive influences that used her as a vessel from which to attack me. I pray on her behalf that her life would be kept from harm; that you would station and strengthen the angels around her to protect her from the evil one. I pray that you would begin now to bring blessings into her life. Heal her relationships from childhood on. Bring her into right relationship with her father and mother, her husband and children [as the case may be], so that through these relationships she may find fulfillment as a woman, security, peace and healing. Bring her health to her body, healing from any diseases that are afflicting her, health to her finances, and reliable people upon whom she can depend for help in time of need. [It is possible that here the Holy Spirit may give you a word of knowledge regarding something specific to pray for. Pray for that also.] And Lord, please pursue and win this woman for Your kingdom. Let her know of Your wonderful love and plan of salvation. Release Your Word into her life. Send messengers and water the seed of Your Word in her life until it springs up into green and tender shoots. Nourish and protect it until it grows fruit. Lead her in paths of righteousness and a rich relationship with You that is as great or greater than the one I have with You.

And Father, if there is to be a (future) relationship for me with this woman while still on this earth, I pray for a relationship which would stand before You and before men as a righteous relationship. Make it one which would meet Your standards as well as those of my wife and my father and mother. Thank you for hearing this request and answering it, making a righteous man out of me according to the model of Your Son, Jesus Christ. In His Name, Amen.

In addition to the above six areas of activity to be exercised on each occasion of attack of your thoughts, it is also important to do two other things *on a regular and continuing basis:*

7. Become accountable for your failures and weaknesses to someone who loves you and for whom your purity is important and who will pray for you. (Husbands, this is preferably your wife. Sons, this is preferably your mother or father. Alternatives could be a pastor or a small support group of men, especially if you are unmarried.) The power you gain over tormenting spirits by merely making yourself accountable to other members of the body of Christ and *taking away the secrecy of their operations* is tremendous. Recognize that accountability is your chief source of protection against any of the enemy's efforts to deceive and bring destructive influences against you. This means confessing your failures and weaknesses to those other special support persons in your life. Learn and apply the following Scriptures to those close to you in the body of Christ for your benefit as well as for them: Hebrews 3:13, James 5:16, Galatians 6:1, Second Timothy 4:2, James 4:6-7.

8. Cleanse the temple of your mind, remembering that Jesus taught that this is necessary to sanctify you and to keep the unclean spirits out (Matt. 12:43-45; John 13:10, 15:3, 6-7, 6:63, 17:17). Give God the use of His own Word for your washing with water and the Word (Eph. 5:26). Learn these specific Scriptures and apply them in personalized form to the enemy whenever he appears in strong temptation: Romans 6:1-14, James 1:1-8, Romans 8:1-14, Philippians 4:4-8. Continue to read and personally implant the Word of God into your life in all areas.

Breaking the mold of the natural man is not easy. He dies hard, but he can be put to death after all. It is the Word of God working in you. *Commencing prayer when you are being buffeted, especially the prayer of item 6 above, will be especially difficult at first.* But as you obediently engage in spiritual warfare according to the above pattern, you will experience the miraculous power of God in ways that cannot be anticipated, marvelous in their reflection of the power and beauty of our Lord Jesus Christ. Thus we experience and share in the true "freedom of the glory of the children of God" for which Christ redeemed us with His blood.

25

Broken Women

Their little ones also will be dashed to pieces
before their eyes; Their houses will be plundered
and their wives ravished.

Isaiah 13:16

How many men would have their wives defiled by other men, their sons and daughters dashed to pieces? We are living in a generation where this is now the rule, not the exception. Over half the men of our nation have either divorced their wives or failed to support the needs of them for whom they promised publicly before God to protect "until death." They failed to protect them from defilement. So much for the "wife of our youth."

It is normal now for pastors to find that half of the women in their congregations are victims of incest or rape. Sodomy, sexual perversion or child molestation are considered normal, because they are so common. It is normal now for daughters raised in so-called Christian families to plan to give away their virginity by age sixteen, or "no later than the Senior Prom." Thus advanced is our degradation in the cesspool of sexual immorality. We are destroying ourselves and our children on our own funeral pyre and sacrifices to Baal!

How many men realize that WE are responsible for the defilement of nearly an entire generation of wives and children? WE are the very defilement of manhood and these are the consequences. There is no escaping the curse, by which the iniquities of the fathers (not "parents," but "fathers"!) are visited upon the children, and on the third and the fourth generations of those who hate the Lord. We have visited these righteous laws of the living God upon those we were tasked to love and protect. We have squandered our manhood on the ground like streams of water in the streets. Our foolishness, selfishness and brokenness knows no bounds. Our filthiness and stench have risen to the heavens. Can God ever redeem us from such squalor?

A report on "Women In Prison" in *Parade Magazine* (April, 1988) reported that 85% of the women in prison are there because they became romantically involved with men who used them. These women were coerced into crime by men they thought they loved. Out of a sense of misguided loyalty or under the threat of injury to themselves or their children they became involved in robbery, extortion, dealing in drugs and a host of other crimes. Can any man comprehend the degree to which women seek identity and fulfillment in men and can be deluded into their own destruction? Who will set them free? Have any of them ever met a real man?

The actress Ava Gardner, one of the most famous sex goddesses of all time, who appeared in 60 major films and had three marriages, including one to Frank Sinatra, died an unfulfilled woman. She said later in life that she'd gladly have traded her career for a lasting marriage: "One good man I could love and marry and cook for and make a home for, who would stick around for the rest of my life" (*USA Today*, Jan. 26-28, 1990). Did she ever meet "one good man"? How would she have recognized him?

We are all broken into pieces and there is only one remedy. We must be born again and have Christ live a new life in us. Only in Him is the good seed of the Father. Only by receiving Him does that seed become planted in us. Only by being baptized into Him can we die to the old nature. Jesus alone is able to live life faithfully, to bring us to the Father to discipline away our foolishness, to bring us onto higher ground, to enable us to live for others. Everything is in Jesus. All healing, all solutions, all restoration, all shortcomings between us and God are made up through Jesus. There is no other solution than Jesus! *None!*

Oh, God, bring our nation to repentance. Deliver us from our iniquities. Bring Christ into the center of our lives. Redeem us from the enemy who destroys us and save our wives and children. Spare us from judgment. Give us a purpose to live — for our families and for You. For Your own sake, dear God, do not leave us in this awful condition. In Thy tender mercy restore to us true manhood — Jesus Christ! Give us purity and purpose to live as Jesus; to find and share abundant life with those whom You place in our care. Give us Your utter faithfulness, that we may be found faithful in that day when there is no sunset and we see only Your glory. Come quickly, Lord Jesus! Amen.

Epilogue: Applications to Healing

He sent His word and healed them...
Psalm 107:20

The bride of Christ is not exempt from the consequences of violating God's laws. Many lives remain scarred and broken because the scriptural precepts of the design and function of men and women discussed in the previous chapters have been broken and have never been reckoned with through the blood of Christ. Do not be deceived. "Your sins will find you out" (Nu. 32:23).

This chapter is purposed to enable the healing of many who require illustrative aids to see clearly how their violation of God's principles has resulted in the bondage of their present unhappiness. Once clear, it is hoped that they will take the matter to God, repent of their sins and place the matter under the blood of Jesus for cleansing and healing.

Among the many problems which are revealed during marriage counseling (nearly 100% of which cases involve premarital sex either with the spouse they later married or with others), one very typical problem is wives who are not bonded to their husbands because they had premarital sex with other men. The result is that, when they have children, they become centered upon their children (through the bonding of childbirth) and find no fulfillment as women in their husbands. In fact, their husbands come to find that they only exist for the purpose of sustaining their wife's ability to raise her children. The husband comes under extreme pressure of his wife to perform economically and will usually experience separation or divorce by the wife if he fails to perform satisfactorily. He is frequently precluded from his normal role as disciplinarian of the children and is blamed for everything which would tend to reduce the mother's fragile self-esteem as a mother. This can be especially devastating if the children further experience debilitating disease or injury, drugs or immorality, and if the mother's self-esteem is totally rooted in her children and not in her husband.

A particularly painful situation is one where the man gives his virginity to a woman who has had many men and marries her, thinking that his forgiveness will heal the problem. It does not. In addition to having given up headship of the family, he wakes up one day to discover that his wife can get along fine without him and there is nothing he can do (outside of Christ) to have her soul to knit to his. In counseling such a situation, it is important to recognize that a man must be persuaded to meet all of his obligations as a husband for the physical, economic and emotional security of the wife before God can be expected to work healing in Christ and fulfillment in the wife. However, God will enable a repentant man to do this.

Husbands who have failed to meet the financial needs of their families usually have need to repent of their sexual violation of their wives prior to the marriage covenant, and frequently of adultery, as well. Both of these sins have opened them to loss of manhood and the legal ravages of satan working against their physical, economic and emotional strength.

The impotence resulting from loss of manhood, loss of headship of family (and failure of the wife to nourish their husbands properly) frequently results in extreme frustration and bitterness of the man toward women and those whom he feels have displaced him from his rightful position, which in turn results in hardness of heart toward God. Counseling and healing requires uncovering and confessing all of the roots of bitterness as well as confrontation with the sins of the man which produced these consequences.

Women who have held their husbands in the bondage of expectations to prove their love to them, due to the consequences of premarital sex, need to be brought to repentance for their failure to remain under adequate protection prior to marriage (their fathers, pastors, etc.), their agreement to commit sin and their role in contributing to the robbing of their husband's manhood and perverting the proper husband-wife relationship. They need to be led to understand that their own well-being depends upon maintaining their husband as a healthy shield. They need to be led in vision-building regarding how they can turn their lives to loving their husbands unconditionally and find new, creative ways of nurturing their physical and emotional needs.

Men who fail to recognize that their livelihood is only a means of ministering economically to their families sometimes overextend themselves in business at the expense of their family's security. In one instance, a young Christian was warned by the author not to mortgage his family's home for the sake of expanding his business, since it jeopardized his family's security in the event something should happen to him. The counsel was not heeded. The home was heavily mortgaged and shortly thereafter his business went into bankruptcy. His wife was forced to go back to work. Then he also contracted cancer, threatening to leave his wife a widow incapable of paying off the house mortgage and raising the children. The Word of God came alive in him, he repented before God and matters of his economic and family priorities were scripturally set straight. The Lord miraculously healed his finances and his body from cancer.

Similar guidance can be given to any man contemplating investments, special gifts to the body of Christ, or career changes. His paramount ministry is to the security of his wife and family.

Great healings as well as discipleship growth and accountability protection have been found in the building of support groups: the formation of a group of three to five persons who meet regularly to surround and build fellowship with one who is weak. Although the fruit becomes multifaceted, providing support and growth in the lives of all participants, it is founded primarily on the principle of building a "three-fold cord" to strengthen the weaker with consistent love, direction and accountability. The group itself needs to be accountable to a pastor or counselor with whom the basic elements of a covenant agreement to carry on this work can be nourished and maintained. The effectiveness of a support group is inherently limited by its faithfulness — which, in turn, will depend upon that level of faithfulness which God has yet established in the strongest member in the chain of accountability (including the pastor, if he is at the head of the chain). Dramatic results have been obtained in a variety of applications, including dealing with manic-depressive illness, broken relationships, unprotected women (using married couples as support groups) and pastoral support. Participants should be both exhorted and warned that commitment to a support group *becomes life-giving through the load-bearing* that takes place as each participant learns to share and bear each other's loads. It is a stressful demand for which leadership should be placed only upon those who are successful in their families (or in their relationships and employment, if single).

Women born out of wedlock or subjected to incest become hosts for spirits of hate and scorn of men (related to the gross failure of their shields), extreme insecurity and controlling, manipulating spirits which demand dominance in any relationship. The latter are essentially indistinguishable from the elementary spirits of witchcraft which also seek to control or manipulate events, people and the future for self-serving purposes. Counseling and healing require identification and renunciation of all these spirits and the closing of their doors of access through forgiveness and the breaking of the curse of the law by the blood of Jesus.

The tremendous number of women in the economic marketplace today are reflections of the inadequacies of men to provide security and opportunities for women to find true fulfillment as wives and mothers and *the opportunities for growth which lie beyond that.* Women have either been forced into the marketplace or obliged to seek better prospects for happiness. Years of effort leave most of them disillusioned and unhappy, subjected to emotional stresses for which they are not designed and attempting to perform many types of work for which they are also not designed. Commonplace sexual immorality and loss of control of their teenage children bring them to shame (Prov. 29:15), and leave them with neither a successful husband nor godly seed with which they can identify. Failure to find an economic base from which to pursue their talents, which God has designed them to develop in relationship to a husband (Prov.31:10-31), leave most modern women who have shunned or discarded husbands without fulfillment even in their God-given talents.

Women who have got as far as admitting they need counseling can usually quickly identify areas in which they are improperly bonded and motivated (through sexual defilement) or have been attempting to operate in areas for which they are not designed.

Experience to date offers great hope for believing young women who have foolishly given away their virginity and come to repentance in Christ over their relationship with their boyfriends. In two instances these precepts were applied to provide accountability to boyfriends who originally had no intention of marrying the girls. Brought to repentance through the gospel of Jesus Christ and sincerely seeking righteous relationships in their lives, the girls submitted to a structured support group of older couples who were able to provide interim guidance on dating criteria and discipline on the young men, which the girls' fathers were unable to provide. The accountability which was brought into the lives of the young men was difficult (requiring "price-paying" by both the counselors and the young men) and produced bonding of the men to their girlfriends.

In other similar instances, the young woman has chosen instead to renounce any relationship with the young man whatsoever. Her bonding has been dissolved and a "spirit of virginity" restored through prayer in company with her pastor and parents, with faith in the power of the blood of Jesus Christ to propitiate all effects of the curse of the law into God's blessings in her life as a believer.

In regard to counseling such cases as girls with ineffective fathers as well as many others where relationships have been broken between the person being counseled and their father (such as men seeking counseling who have unstable employment patterns and an inability to subordinate their attitudes to their bosses), special attention needs to be focused on the broken relationships with fathers. Significant healing and further protection in the life of the person being counseled requires that they be reconciled and build good relationships with their fathers. In a larger, more general sense, it is the author's opinion that the grace of God given to the counselor (for wisdom and power to disciple someone in Christ) will be inherently limited to that which can enable the person being counseled (man, woman or child) to be reconciled with their parents, if they are still living. The reason for this is that the parent remains one of God's chief sources of authority and guidance in the life of the person being counseled, especially in the life of a man or one yet unmarried. Any assumption by the counselor that he or she has more God-given insight into the life of the person being counseled than their parents is one that usurps the proper position of the parents, who have God-given preeminence over the counselor. Hence, counsel which exceeds these bounds tends to be self-exalting, fails to carry the authority to break strongholds in the life of the person being counseled and is likely destined for failure. The counseling relationship will either stop bearing the fruit of discipleship or the person being counseled will "bolt" from the relationship when its demands reach the same levels which caused previous failure with the parents. To counter this, the counselor must set the tone by his own actions to "honor the parents" (Eph. 6:1-3). Both parties must be alert to expect "counselor rejection" if the opposing strongholds are not first breached and to have a clear understanding that reconciliation with parents, especially fathers, is a centerpiece of the counseling agenda.

Behold, I am going to send you Elijah the prophet before the coming of the great and terrible day of the Lord. And he will restore the hearts of the fathers to their children and the hearts of the children to their fathers, lest I come and smite the land with a curse.

Malachi 4:5-7

Books by Karl Duff

Restoration of Men (God's Rescue of Women and Children)

God provides healing, restoration, and protective accountability for men who find themselves ineffectual as husbands and fathers.

Lord and Scoutmaster

The author relates humorous as well as educational true life adventures he had as a Scout and then as a Scoutmaster.

Leader's Guide for High Adventure

This is a booklet of practical tips for leading Scouts or youth groups on extended backpacking or canoeing trips.

Still the Master of the Sea

With signs and wonders God intervened in a modern hydrofoil warship program and changed a prideful naval officer.

Teens, Sex, and Happiness

God's design of male-female relationships is an important part of His plan for our lives. Youth must obey God's plan to find happiness and fulfillment.

To order additional books, contact the author at:

Karl Duff
6112 Wynn Jones Road East
Port Orchard, WA 98366
206-871-1265

Place this order form in an envelope along with your check or money order.

Qty.	Description	Unit Price	Total Price
	Restoration of Men	$6.95	
	Lord and Scoutmaster	$6.95	
	Leader's Guide for High Adventure	$3.00	
	Still the Master of the Sea	$8.95	
	Teens, Sex, and Happiness	$6.95	

Ship. (quant.)	1-2	3-5	6-9	10-14	15-19	20-25	Subtotal	
Ship. Cost	$2.50	$4.00	$6.50	$10.50	$13.25	$16.00	Less Discount	
							Plus Shipping	
							TOTAL DUE	

Name _____

Address _____

City/State/ZIP _____ Phone # _____

Signature _____ Date _____

20% discount for 5 or more copies